Linguistics, Computers, and the Language Teacher

A Communicative Approach

John H. Underwood

Mills College

NEWBURY HOUSE PUBLISHERS, INC.
ROWLEY, MASSACHUSETTS 01969
ROWLEY • LONDON • TOKYO

1984

Library of Congress Cataloging in Publication Data

Underwood, John H. (John Harvey), 1944–
   Linguistics, computers, and the language teacher.

   Revision of thesis (doctoral)--University of
California, Los Angeles, 1981.
   Includes bibliographies and index.
   1. Language and languages--Computer-assisted
instruction. 2. Communicative competence. I. Title.
P53.28.U53   1984   418'.007'8   84-1102
ISBN 0-88377-470-4

NEWBURY HOUSE PUBLISHERS, INC.

Language Science
Language Teaching
Language Learning

ROWLEY, MASSACHUSETTS 01969
ROWLEY • LONDON • TOKYO

Chapter Seven originally appeared as "Simulated Conversation as a CAI Strategy" in
Foreign Language Annals 15.3, May 1982. Permission to reprint this article in its present
revised form has been granted by the American Council on the Teaching of Foreign
Languages, Inc.

First printing: October 1984

Printed in the U.S.A.   5   4   3   2

For Bego, John, and Cristina

Contents

PART ONE
Language Teaching: Theory and Practice

Preface

The first draft of this book was my doctoral dissertation (1981), written under the supervision of Carlos Otero and Carlos Quicoli of the University of California, Los Angeles. To say that much has happened in computer-assisted language learning since then is an obvious understatement: the most frequently cited references in Part Two had not even been written when I began my research. Yet the problem I point out in my thesis remains critical: the vast majority of foreign language computer programs are still behaviorist drill-and-practice exercises that are neither good pedagogy nor good use of the computer. We need very badly to take a long, critical look at what we are doing, particularly when most of the significant literature on teaching methods now stresses the importance of communicative activities and meaningful practice.

I do not pretend to be impartial. I believe strongly in the arguments I present here, and I try to support my beliefs with sound linguistic and pedagogical theory. If at times I sound overly critical, it is because I believe there is much to be lost by using computers in an uncritical, unthinking manner. Computer critics will argue, not without reason, that machines "trivialize" language learning. To this I would respond that software authors, some of them, have indeed trivialized language learning, but that it need not be so. The purpose of this book is to provide reasons, and directions, for pursuing alternatives.

No project of this sort is ever completed without help of various kinds. I am indebted, as will be clear, to the work of Noam Chomsky, Stephen Krashen, Tracy Terrell, Earl Stevick, Karl Diller, and John Higgins, among others. I wish to thank Professors Otero and Quicoli and Professor Terence Wilbur for their many helpful comments on early versions of the thesis. I also wish to thank Karl Diller for reading and commenting on the thesis; Earl Stevick, John Schumann, Betty Reveley, Abbey Asher, and two anonymous reviewers for comments on drafts of the present book, and Elizabeth Lantz for her constant editorial assistance. Carol Lennox, Vicki O'Day, and Sarah Tyrell provided tireless help and encouragement with the PDP-11 at Mills College, enabling me to write and edit the manuscript with the text-editing program NROFF.

Thanks, too, to those who contributed in less specific ways: my colleagues, my parents, and especially my wife, Bego, who provided invaluable input and who took over many of my responsibilities so that this project could be completed. Finally, I wish to thank my children for being patient—and for keeping me going ("Daddy, what chapter are you on now?").

Oakland, California   J. H. U.
April 1984

Foreword

by Earl W. Stevick

In recent years, two trends have caught the imagination of language teachers. One is the growing emphasis on *communication*—on using language for purposes beyond merely getting the right answer and pleasing the teacher. Communicative teaching concentrates on genuine exchange of information, on games and other self-rewarding activities, and on lively simulations of real and interesting encounters. The second trend is *computer-assisted instruction,* which takes a piece of equipment whose IQ is exactly zero and puts it at the service of the human mind. How can these two trends—toward fully engaging the intelligence of the student, and toward use of equipment that is spectacularly lacking in intelligence—converge to the benefit of language teaching and learning? That is the question that John Underwood addresses in this book.

Underwood builds his answer deliberately and with admirable care. The first part of the book hardly mentions computers. Instead, it is devoted to a treatment of current views of language teaching, and of various communicative methods. Emphasis is given to the distinction between *learning* in the narrow academic sense, and *acquisition* of a second language in ways that resemble a child's acquisition of its first language.

Chapter 6 is for me the center of the book. It begins with a list of 13 premises for communicative applications of computer-assisted language learning, reminiscent of Terrell and Krashen's "Natural Approach." The remainder of the book gives numerous illustrations of how these premises can be applied, and then introduces the reader to the fundamentals of computer use.

As a long-time Luddite who nevertheless admits to a keen interest in the potential of computers for language learning, I am glad that Underwood began his book in the area that I am most familiar with, and led me step-by-step via the software to the hardware. Perhaps other language teachers will also find this strategy to be congenial. All readers will be grateful for the clarity and vigor of the writing.

Arlington, Virginia
March 1984

Introduction

The scene is a workshop on computer-assisted instruction (CAI) at a statewide conference for foreign language teachers. It is a large room, with a battery of TRS-80's along one side, Atari 800's along the other, and Apple II's across the front. With a little pushing and shoving, the teachers are eagerly trying to get up to the keyboards to try out the latest technology in foreign language teaching. When they finally do get their chance, more than one looks around at no one in particular with a puzzled expression and asks, "Is that all they can do?"

No, it is not all they can do. It is because I believe that we can do better than that, that there is more to educational computing than "Hangman" and drill-and-practice, that I am writing this book. We are at a crucial stage in the use of this new technology. From here we could go sailing off blithely in the wrong direction and waste enormous amounts of time and money. Or we could start investing our efforts in a truly useful and intellectually exciting new tool, one that could change the way we think about language teaching. The question at this time, says a program officer at the National Endowment for the Humanities who has been looking into such matters, "is not one of evaluating what is out there—because there isn't much—but of deciding what ought to be done" (Lyn White, quoted in Desruisseaux 1983).

The purpose of this book is to offer a principled basis for deciding "what ought to be done." To do so, we will have to look at a lot more than just computers. First we will have to consider what language learning and teaching are all about: what works, what doesn't, and why. This will be the subject of Part One. We will find that both the theoreticians and the teachers are stressing "communicative competence" as the goal for language teaching. By this they mean the ability to actually use linguistic skills to communicate an appropriate message in a given social context—a far cry from drill-and-practice. In Part Two we will examine what is being done, and could be done, with computers in language teaching, and see how well it fits (or doesn't fit) the premises of Part One. From there we will be able to draw several conclusions and make suggestions for ways to proceed.

Information about language learning and teaching comes from four sources, two theoretical and two practical. From theoretical linguistics we get (1) knowledge about language itself (is it a skill like riding a bicycle or more like doing multiplication?), and (2) knowledge about language acquisition, how humans learn or otherwise "get" language. These will be the topics of Chapters 1 and 2, respectively. On the practical side, we have the insights gained from (3) classroom experience and experimentation, including the intriguing discoveries that have come from trying out new methods, and (4) applied linguistic research (comparing methods). Both of these areas will be covered in Chapter 3, the latter only briefly, a full review of the research being beyond the scope of this book.

The discussion of computers in Part Two will begin with a brief review in Chapter 4 of the rise and fall of the language lab, an important moral lesson in the use and misuse of technology. We will see that the lab does in fact have at least one important communicative function—listening comprehension practice. Chapter 5 will consider what is currently being done in computer-assisted language learning (CALL). We will try out some of the existing programs and critique them by holding them up to the language teaching principles from Part One; most of them will not score well.

Chapter 6 is the heart of the matter. Looking for alternatives to the "wrong-try-again" approach dominating current software, we will discover a number of innovative programs which seem very promising indeed. To these we will add suggestions for other possible "communicative" programs, plus a look at the potential for incorporating sound and pictures. In Chapter 7 we will look at "artificially intelligent" programs, including an experimental communicative Spanish program that may or may not suggest where we should be going from here. Finally, in Chapter 8 we will consider how one might get started: the feasibility of writing one's own software, some guidelines for those who choose to do so, plus guidelines for evaluating other people's software. We will conclude on a philosophical note: "Should we be doing CALL at all?"

This is, I want to make clear, primarily a book about language teaching. It is intended both for language teachers (including ESL teachers) who may have experimented with, or thought about experimenting with, using computers in their teaching, and for those who are merely curious—perhaps even skeptical—about the whole business. It is also clearly directed at software developers or programmers who are considering going into foreign language software and who need very badly to understand what our profession is all about. It is not a research report on experiments comparing CAI and non-CAI classes. I think it is too early for that. We need first to reflect more on the language learning process, look at what is going on in the classroom, and then ask some hard questions: Does the computer help us accomplish what we are trying to do? Does that $39.95 program actually do anything related to the goals we have set for our students? Or have we developed yet another form of electronic babysitting?

We are clearly entering an exciting era, although not without a certain amount of fear and trembling. Machiavelli expressed our situation very well:

> There is nothing more difficult to take in hand, more perilous to conduct, or more uncertain in its success, than to take the lead in the introduction of a new order of things (*The Prince,* VI).

If there is a message running through this book, it is that we—language teachers—must take the lead. We who understand best what it means to teach and learn a language will have to make it clear what we want, and what we don't want, from the software people. We must not allow our ignorance or timidity of technology to cause us to sell out our principles, our beliefs about what is good and right and sensible in our profession. If we say nothing, the computer people will give us what they think we want, or what is easy to program, or what they have always done. This is the time for the language teaching profession to make a principled statement about "what ought to be done."

Linguistics, Computers, and the Language Teacher

one

Language Teaching: Theory and Practice

The ability to construct for oneself an abstract grammar of underlying principles is a unique human endowment, a fundamental characteristic of human intelligence. It is the task of the teacher to construct the conditions under which this natural human ability will be put to use. (Chomsky 1969, 13)

chapter

1

Theory: Chomsky's View of Language

For years it was assumed that linguistics, the scientific study of language, would have much to say to the language teacher. In fact, the term *applied linguistics* was often used as a virtual synonym for "language teaching." Some teachers felt that linguistics would provide the answer to all their problems. Others were never that convinced. For many, in fact, linguistics was just "a vast unknown land peopled by creatures who speak gibberish to one another and who occasionally leave their esoteric labors to point an accusing finger at the language teaching profession" (Axelrod 1966).

Yet there clearly should be some connection. There are at least two areas of linguistic study that would seem to have something to say to us: (1) The theory of language itself, or "theoretical linguistics," because it can give us insight into the kind of skill we are trying to impart, and (2) perhaps more important, the theory of how people learn or acquire language, which is part of what is known as "psycholinguistics." In this chapter we will consider the first of these; the latter will be discussed in Chapter 2.[1]

3

1.1 THEORETICAL LINGUISTICS: GENERATIVE GRAMMAR

Theoretical linguistics has been largely dominated in the last twenty years by the work of Noam Chomsky and his followers. Chomsky's *Syntactic Structures* in 1957 and his review of Skinner's *Verbal Behavior* in 1959 drastically changed our way of looking at language. This new school of linguistics, variously known as transformational, generative, or transformational-generative (TG) grammar, attracted a considerable following and generated an impressive amount of research into grammatical theory, especially syntax and phonology. It is still strong today, in the form of what is known as the Extended Standard Theory.

It is no more possible to describe TG theory in a paragraph or two than it is to do justice to the theory of relativity in the same space. Yet we should be familiar with a few basic notions of the theory if for no nother reason than that they have clear implications for what we are doing: (1) the concept of different levels of structure, (2) the function of transformations, (3) the distinction between competence and performance, and (4) the view of language as rule-governed creativity. In the following section, we examine these notions, especially the last, and their implications for language teaching.

1.2 IMPLICATIONS OF GENERATIVE THEORY

1.2.1 Language Has More Than One Level of Structure

Prior to TG grammar, linguists describing sentences tended to assume that "what you see is what you get": the structure of a sentence was all perfectly visible, and when more than one sentence showed the same obvious structure, one could describe it as a "pattern." Yet this clearly was not the whole story. In his now famous examples, Chomsky pointed out that "John is easy to please" seems to have the same structure as "John is eager to please," and yet any native speaker knows that somehow the relationship of John to the act of pleasing is quite different. Chomsky described the situation as two accidentally similar "surface structures" with different "deep" or "underlying" structures. This explains, he pointed out, how it is possible that one sentence can somehow mean two different things (i.e., be ambiguous), as in "Visiting relatives can be boring," which can mean either "Relatives who visit can be boring" or "To visit relatives can be boring."

It is a very revealing distinction, and one that says a lot to the language teacher. First because it gives us a way of explaining to ourselves why it is that superficial similarities in sentences often hide the real facts of their meanings. More important is how it can affect the sentences we choose for classroom presentation or practice. To understand this, you need only imagine a drill for practicing the pattern: Noun Phrase + *is* + Adjective + Infinitive in which the following sentences are lumped together:

English is hard to learn
Mary is ready to go
Milk is good to drink
The teacher is pleased to meet you

"Structure signals its own meaning," pre-Chomskyan linguists used to say. True, if you go below the surface. The structures here are signaling two different meanings, as shown by the way they can (or cannot) be paraphrased with *it*:[2]

It is hard to learn English
*It is ready to go Mary
It is good to drink milk
*It is pleased to meet you the teacher

These structures thus cannot be taught in any meaningful way without having these different meanings pointed out.

1.2.2 Transformations Change Structures into Other Structures

When two sentences with differing surface structures appear to have the same meaning, it is often the case that they "come from" (in a technical sense we need not worry about here) the same deep structure, but through the application of different rules, called transformations, which move, delete, or add words. To take a simple example, any speaker of English knows that "John turned off the radio" and "John turned the radio off" are in some sense the same. When linguists suggest that these two sentences come from the same deep structure and that the particle *off* has simply been moved by a transformation (known as Particle Shift), they not only describe the facts, but they also give us a hypothesis to explain how it is that we native speakers know these are the same—quite simply, we know the rule (albeit unconsciously). In the same way, we know that although we can say "John turned it off," we cannot say (with normal stress) "*John turned off it." How do we know that? One theory: because we know that Particle Shift is obligatory when the direct object is a pronoun.

One of the revealing insights of TG for language teachers is just how complex these rules can be. The rule that derives the question "Can you speak English?" from "You can speak English" is a relatively simple inversion known as Subject-Auxiliary-Inversion (SAI). But English questions, unlike questions in Spanish, for example, are not always that easy. Consider what happens in "Harry likes pizza"—"Does Harry like pizza?" or in a "wh" question such as "What does Harry like?" This last question involves three transformations: WH-Movement (*what* goes to the front), *Do* Insertion (note there is no *do* in the original declarative), and SAI (assuming *do* is an auxiliary like *can,* it must be moved in front of the subject). In addition to all this, the speaker has to be sure that the form of *do* agrees with the subject. For teachers, these facts provide a strong argument in favor of treating questions with *can* and questions with *do* in a very different way.

1.2.3 Knowing Rules Is Not the Same as Using Them

As complicated as these transformations may seem at times, as native speakers we clearly know them in that intuitive and unconscious way we know something we cannot explain. Most native speakers of course cannot explain why they don't say "*John turned off it"—"it just doesn't sound right." This knowledge Chomsky calls "linguistic competence." It is a kind of theoretical knowledge in the sense that it makes it possible for us to produce an infinite series of perfectly grammatical sentences, except that they don't always come out that way. What comes out is "performance," sometimes hesitant or interrupted, often ungrammatical simply because we forgot what we were saying. (Consider the common extra preposition in things like "*This is exactly the goal for which we have all been working so hard for.")

The language teacher would do well to remember that although linguistic competence clearly is what we ultimately are working for, what we see on a day-to-day basis is performance. When our students' performance gets ragged, we may be tempted to simply patch it up in some more or less superficial way and go on. Yet, as Stevick points out, that may be too easy. We need to ask ourselves at that point how we can change what they know, not just what they do, although what they do will certainly give us a strong clue to what they know (Stevick 1982, 13).

1.2.4. Language Is Rule-Governed Creativity

Underlying any discussion of the relationship between language theory and language teaching is a simple and often overlooked fact: implicitly or explicitly, anything we do in the language classroom is based on an assumed definition of language. The audiolingual method ("mim/mem" and pattern drill) is based on a very limited and mechanical conception of language, as a type of stimulus-response behavior: "whenever a person speaks," said Hockett, "he is either mimicking or analogizing" (Hockett 1958, 425). By "analogizing," Hockett apparently means something akin to "slot substitution." He gives the example of children producing plurals such as *mans* and *sheeps* on the analogy of all the regular plurals they have heard.

What generative grammar gives us is a rich, humanistic view of language as the creative use of internalized rules. In this view the child produces forms such as *mans* or *sheeps* by applying an acquired rule for plural formation. Thus when we speak we create new sentences by employing those unconscious rules we carry around in our heads. This means that with only a small number (a "finite set") of the kind of rules we have been discussing, we can create an endless number (an "infinite set") of entirely new sentences, sentences never before spoken, just as we can understand any number of sentences we have never heard before. This is a very powerful and open-ended view of human language; if language were a mere set of conditional responses to stimuli produced by a "situational context," it would be difficult indeed to explain this power. There is, says Chomsky, "no known sense of 'generalization' that can begin to account for this characteristic 'creative' aspect of language use" (Chomsky 1966, 44).

The implications for the language teacher are far-reaching. If using language means the creative application of unconscious rules, then language practice (if it is aimed at helping students use the language for themselves rather than merely parrot it) must be practice in doing just that—using rules to create meaningful utterances, to communicate. In this view, then, there can be little value in having students memorize or repeat sentences which someone else has created, which mean nothing to them, and which do not communicate any real "here and now" message. Memorizing dialogs or the meaningless repetition of pattern drills is thus, at best, highly questionable. Chomsky's position on drill is unequivocal: "There can be nothing more stultifying than language drill, whether it is mere memorization of paradigms or the mindless repetition of patterns divorced from any meaningful context" (Chomsky 1969, 6).

The key word here is "meaningful." Partly because of the influence of the TG model, we are seeing ever-increasing efforts to make classroom activities meaningful and communicative.[3] This means allowing and encouraging students to create their own sentences, to somehow talk about what they want to talk about and not just what the book would have them say. Furthermore, students must always know what they are saying—not just what the whole utterance means, but how the various parts mean what they do. It is through perceived meaning, or changes in meaning, that they can begin to form those all-important internalized rules of grammar. One abstract grammatical structure is only perceived to be different from another if it is associated with a perceptible difference in meaning. "Unless we can link the structure to the meaning," says Diller, "there is no use in being able to produce the structure. To learn how to form the past tense of the verb, we talk about what we did yesterday. To learn the present perfect tense, we talk about what we have done in the last several weeks" (Diller 1978, 36).

Of course, with all this "innovation" and "creative" practice, there will be mistakes. In the habit-formation theory, mistakes were fatal, to be avoided at all costs, since clearly they could only lead to the formation of bad habits. It was this fear that led to the total control of the pattern drill. In the TG model, we realize that mistakes must be made in order for students to test hypotheses about the rules they are starting to form in their heads. In fact, they provide the teacher with clues to the present state of the student's competence, and suggest how much more needs to be done. And we realize that when practice emphasizes meaning, when the student is making an effort to convey a message, to interrupt with a correction would mean abruptly switching the emphasis back to form—and probably destroying the feeling of real communication we have tried to foster. This leads to a considerably more relaxed attitude toward classroom errors (indeed, in Chapter 2 we will see arguments that, in most cases, they should not be corrected at all). "No language teacher," says Jakobovits, "should ever force his pupils to use only well-formed sentences in practice conversation, whether it be in the classroom, laboratory or outside" (1968, 107). Adds Chastain, "[They] do not speak their own language perfectly, and the chances are that they will not speak the second language perfectly either. The important point is that they feel free to participate and to speak" (1976, 337). Such statements are sometimes seen as condoning a permissive attitude toward ungrammaticality. We must maintain the distinction between our long-range goal of socially acceptable speech and our short-term need to adopt realistic standards for the learner whose language is in a state of development.

Drill, especially manipulative drill (as opposed to communicative drill, where the material is somewhat contextualized), is clearly of only limited use. That leaves dialogs, the memorization part of the audiolingual method. The idea was to memorize a good-sized chunk of "authentic," i.e., natural and native-like, language as a kind of mental phrasebook, phrases that could then be extended through the analogizing of pattern practice. Of course dialogs once again are prefabricated language, someone else's speech, and ironically all the time spent practicing this authentic language is that much less time for saying anything "real," for communication. Although some learners do manage to generalize from canned material to real conversation, there is no evidence that the average learner can readily adopt strategies for doing so.

1.3 PROBLEMS WITH GENERATIVE THEORY

Much of what we have just said has been the subject of considerable misunderstanding. In the early years, educational popularizations of transformational work, or "applied TG," were frequently based on mis-readings or trivializations. Typical was the sudden popularity of transfor-mational drills (transforming statements to questions, affirmatives to negatives, etc.) in the language classroom; many writers mistakenly argued that TG provided a new rationale for practicing such manipulation. Other popularizers invented implausible transformational "rules" to describe linguistic facts, thereby obscuring both the facts and the theoreti-cal model they were supposedly using. In fact, the whole notion of a rule of grammar was very often misread. While for Chomsky rules are the internalized competence of the native speaker, many teachers assumed he meant the overt, how-to-do-it rules, like "always use *whom* after a preposition." In fact, such rules would come under the heading of what we call "prescriptive grammar," a generally unscientific set of guidelines or "linguistic etiquette."

Much misunderstanding came from simply assuming that "descriptive grammars" and "teaching grammars" were one and the same thing. Yet clearly what is valid for analysis may not be at all appropriate for preparing teaching materials, even less for classroom presentation. The teacher is tempted, Newmark explains, to use generative grammar in language teaching materials because it offers elegant grammatical descriptions, ordered rules that suggest (incorrectly, more often than not) a sequence for presentation, and of course the ubiquitous "transformational" drills, which are so easy to use. But, he warns, "these appeals are deceptive . . . the ordering of rules is based on theoretical principles, not pedagogical ones" (Newmark 1966, 217).

As a simple example, the generative grammarian might describe indirect discourse (reported speech) in terms of "embedded sentences." Thus a sentence such as

(1)   John says he's going to be a little late

might be shown, in one analysis, to be derived from something like

(2)   John says [that [John's going to be a little late]]

i.e., a sentence within a sentence, by means of some sort of pronoun substitution rule. In a teaching grammar, on the other hand, it would almost certainly be more useful to relate (1) to its direct discourse counterpart:

(3)   John says, "I'm going to be a little late"

since (3) can be handily converted into (1) by simply asking the student, "What does John say?," without needing to refer to the relatively abstract and perhaps confusing structure in (2).

A teaching grammar is thus not just a simplified model of a theoretical grammar, but one that must answer its own questions and develop its own way of doing things. Rivers (1976, 11) points out that, although a descriptive grammar offers insight into the subject matter, the "what" to teach, the teaching grammar must seek the most psychologically appropriate way of arranging and presenting the material to the students; i.e., the "how." This will depend on a variety of factors, including course objectives, age, and intellectual maturity of the students; intensity and length of study; and the degree of contrast between the native language and the target language.

The crucial misunderstanding about TG is a more basic one, however. As Krashen puts it, it is "the failure to understand that a theory of grammatical structure and language universals is not necessarily the same as a theory of language acquisition" (Krashen 1983, 53). TG, he says, is a theory of the *product,* the adult's competence, rather than a theory of the *process* by which the adult has acquired that competence (Krashen 1982, 6). (This process is the subject of Chapter 2.) It is thus not surprising, he argues, that all those attempts at "applied TG" would fail to make any significant contribution to language teaching.

This is very much what Chomsky seemed to be trying to say in his famous statement of "skepticism" in the Northeast Conference paper (Chomsky 1966): the theory could not offer any quick-fix applications or support a "technology" of language teaching (his suggestions on techniques, as we have seen, were mostly negative). But he did envision a basic approach consistent with his view of language:

> All we can suggest is that a teaching program be designed in such a way as to give free play to those creative principles that humans bring to the process of language learning. I think we should probably try to create a rich linguistic environment for the intuitive heuristics that the normal human automatically possesses.

This gives us much to think about. In fact, as Blair points out, it leaves us with two decidedly nontrivial questions: What is a "rich linguistic environment," and how can we create such an environment in our classrooms? (Blair 1982, 14). Much of the discussion of second language acquisition theory in Chapter 2 centers on a hypothesis which, if true, will provide an answer to the first question. The second question finds several different kinds of answers in the discussion of methods in Chapter 3.

1.4 SUMMARY: WHAT THE THEORY TELLS US

The transformational generative model provides us with a view of the richness, complexity, and creativity of human language. It tells us that language is not a set of habits to be mindlessly drilled, but the creative use of internalized rules. These rules are complex and abstract and do not lend themselves easily to conscious formulation, but constitute instead our unconscious "competence" which makes it possible to generate an infinite array of new sentences. The model tells us, furthermore, that if language use is creation rather than analogy, language practice should involve creation rather than analogy, i.e., communicative practice with focus on meaning rather than structural practice with focus on form. Focusing on meaning implies the avoidance of prefabricated speech, memorized dialogs, or similar manipulative practice. Finally, errors will tend to be played down; in communicative practice, especially, they will not be corrected, because to do so would be to switch the focus from meaning to form.

In Chapter 2 we will discover that current research in second language acquisition has arrived at a set of hypotheses, what I will call "The Input Model," which has implications for the language teacher that are remarkably similar to those we have just outlined.

NOTES TO CHAPTER 1

1. There is a third area of linguistics that is equally important, although perhaps less central, to our discussion here. Research in "descriptive linguistics" gives us exacting and explicit analyses of language facts which can show us the inner workings of the languages we teach. (In Chapter 7 we will see how an explicit statement of the facts concerning the verbs SER and ESTAR in Spanish is essential to the development of a computer program designed to practice the problem.)

2. The asterisk will be used throughout to denote ungrammatical utterances, i.e., something the native speaker of the language would not say.

3. The concept of meaningful practice is of course hardly new. In Fries's classic manual on teaching English as a foreign language (Fries 1945), although his drills are aimed at habit formation, he cautions against "artificiality," recommending that exercises be as relevant as possible to the student's actual life. Unfortunately, however, later structuralist texts tended to ignore Fries's commendable advice.

chapter

2

Theory: The Input Model of Acquisition

In Chapter 2, we examined the question "What is language?" in light of current linguistic theory, specifically the transformational-generative model. Nevertheless, as we have seen, the answers tell us more about the product than about the process by which it is acquired. The process is the concern of that part of linguistics known as "second language acquisition theory." Although there are actually several theories, the one that appears to have the clearest pedagogical implications at the present time, and therefore has attracted the most attention among language teachers, is that of Stephen Krashen. Based on the work of a number of researchers, Krashen has proposed a set of hypotheses sometimes known as "The Monitor Theory" or "The Monitor Model"; I refer to it here as "The Input Model," since I feel it is the input hypothesis that best summarizes what it is all about.

The version of the theory outlined in Krashen (1982) has five parts: (1) the distinction between acquisition and learning, (2) the natural order hypothesis, (3) the Monitor hypothesis, (4) the input hypothesis, and (5) the affective filter hypothesis.

2.1 THE DISTINCTION BETWEEN ACQUISITION AND LEARNING

We have become accustomed to describing the way we got our first language as "acquisition," whereas we use the term "learning" for what older children and adults do in the language classroom. Thus it was assumed that children "acquire" a language, whereas adults can only "learn"—that somehow the "language acquisition device" (LAD), to use Chomsky's term, shut down somewhere around puberty. Now researchers are saying that this is not entirely true, that in fact the LAD apparently does not shut down, and that adults may be capable of both learning (in this restricted sense) and acquiring language.

Learning is "conscious knowledge of a second language, knowing the rules in the sense of being aware of them, and being able to talk about them" (Krashen 1982, 10), what we commonly call "knowing about" a language as opposed to "knowing" it. Learning, of course, is most of what goes on in the foreign language classroom when we are focusing on form rather than on meaning. (I will henceforth use the term "learning" in this restricted sense.)

Acquisition, on the other hand, is much like the way we got our first language, i.e., through exposure to language we can understand. It is subconscious, with attention to meaning rather than form: "Language acquirers are not usually aware of the fact that they are acquiring language, but are only aware of the fact that they are using the language for communication" (Krashen 1982, 10). Material is presented as in conversation, with no special attention to new items, no drilling, no grammar explanation. In short, it is what we commonly call "picking up" a language. The end result is Chomsky's "competence"—unconscious, tacit knowledge of the rules of grammar, rules that we cannot express, but that enable us to produce well-formed sentences.

The crucial difference is in the way students use the two kinds of knowledge. Acquisition leads to the ability to use a language to communicate. Learning leads primarily to the ability to monitor or edit what we are saying or writing—if in fact there is enough time to put it to use, and if we have the rule straight in our heads. (We will see soon how this Monitor works.) This means, in turn, that correcting students' mistakes, since it diverts their attention from the meaning to the form, mainly affects learning, i.e., it contributes to the Monitor; corrections are apparently of little help in acquisition.

The implications of this distinction for language teaching should be obvious. Says Earl Stevick, one of the most respected writers on foreign language teaching, it is "potentially the most fruitful concept for language teachers that has come out of the linguistic sciences during my professional lifetime" (1980, 270). Why? Because all these years, we have been unwittingly concentrating on trying to get our students to "learn," when what we wanted them to do was "acquire." We were using learning activities when we could have been using acquisition activities. What they did acquire through this process (some a little more than others) was purely accidental, occurring, according to the hypothesis, only because our learning-centered instruction also incidentally provided understandable input. Insofar as students understood what they were drilling, the drill itself would be a source of input. And every time we interrupted our formal lesson plan to tell our students (in the target language) something relating to the real world, even if nothing more than an observation on a point of grammar, we were contributing to their acquisition. In fact, these "interruptions" were quite possibly more useful than the lesson itself.

Finally, note that when this distinction is juxtaposed with the view of language in Chapter 1, we are forced to an interesting conclusion. Language, in Chomsky's view, means the creative application of internalized rules. It is clear now that these must be acquired rules, not learned rules, since what we have acquired can be used to create utterances, whereas what we have learned cannot. There is thus a sense in which what we have learned, whatever it is, cannot be "language" in Chomsky's terms. Conclusion: whenever we have been drilling grammatical form, we may have been teaching grammar, but not, strictly speaking, "language."

2.2 THE NATURAL ORDER HYPOTHESIS

Language teaching materials are usually arranged in some sort of sequence, normally in order of assumed grammatical difficulty. Language acquisition research now shows that in fact a natural order exists for the acquisition of certain grammatical structures, for both first and second language. Although the order for second language acquisition is not the same as for the first, the interesting discovery is that different groups of second language acquirers show a remarkably similar order. For example, in acquiring morphemes in English, -*ing* is normally developed before the possessive -*'s,* irregular past tense before regular, etc. (Krashen 1982, 12). That is, left to their own devices, nonnatives will "pick up" grammar much in this order.

It would be tempting to conclude that we should therefore teach according to this natural order, but that is not Krashen's point. In fact, as long as our goal is acquisition rather than learning, he would have us reject grammatical sequencing altogether. Precisely because the language acquirer will develop grammar according to a built-in natural order, we should not attempt to second-guess the acquirer and tinker with this order. There are other disadvantages to a grammatical syllabus: it assumes all students are at the same stage of acquisition, it normally means presenting each structure only once, it leads to deliberately "contextualized" materials that tend to prevent natural communication, and it assumes that we know far more than we do about the order in which we acquire language (Krashen 1982, 70). Krashen argues instead for providing "comprehensible input" rich enough in structure that it will provide all students with an opportunity for unconscious acquisition, along with a good deal of natural review, while attention is focused on the communication of ideas, not on structures (ibid.). We will take a closer look at what he means by "comprehensible input" in our discussion of the input hypothesis.

2.3 THE MONITOR HYPOTHESIS

As we have seen, what we have "learned" and what we have "acquired" differ not only in the way we get them, but also in how we use them. According to the theory, to initiate communication we can use only what we have acquired. What we have learned provides the Monitor with a means of editing or correcting what comes out. Thus rules learned consciously through formal instruction play only a relatively limited role in language production.

The Monitor turns out to be even more limited in that it can only be used under restricted circumstances. We must (1) know the rule (which can be very complex, as we saw in Chapter 1), (2) be thinking consciously about form (rather than about what we are saying, which is more likely), and (3) have enough time to reflect on these things (not normally the case in conversation). On the whole, the Monitor has more chance of being used during a grammar quiz or while writing a composition than during any communicative oral practice. This may explain why students who get 100 percent on a grammar quiz promptly "forget" the same rules during conversation practice immediately afterwards—they have not forgotten, they simply do not have time to use their Monitor. In fact, Krashen concludes that "for most people, even university students, it takes a real discrete-point grammar-type test to meet all three conditions for Monitor use" (Krashen 1982, 18). Students may "learn" rules through drill, practice, and explanation, and they may be able to demonstrate that they "know" these rules on grammar tests, but this knowledge will be of little use to them anywhere else—especially (crucially) in normal communicative situations.

2.4 THE INPUT HYPOTHESIS

We have seen that acquisition is unconscious, whereas learning is conscious; that acquisition follows a natural order; and that conscious grammar has only a rather limited role as Monitor of output. We have still not fully addressed the question of how acquisition takes place; if acquisition is in fact our goal, the question is essential. The input hypothesis claims that language results from "comprehensible input"—

exposure to spoken or written language that we understand and that contains elements at a stage slightly more advanced than our own, stage i + 1, assuming we are at stage i. That is, it must contain structures that are a little beyond our current level of (acquired) competence, structures that we can "reach for" and, in the process, make our own. Crucially, we must understand these new structures. How do we do that if we have not yet acquired them? We understand them from the context, from extralinguistic information (pictures, objects, gestures, etc.), and from the careful way the input is selected and delivered.

Note that this turns traditional foreign language teaching on its head. Instead of teaching structures and then practicing them in communication activities, the hypothesis would have us do the communication first; structure, in its own time, will follow. One student's i + 1 will not be the same as the next's, but with enough data, it will all be there. Of course there will be a rough sequencing of material, otherwise nothing would be understood. But we need not—in fact, should not—make deliberate attempts at i + 1 (recall the arguments against grammatical sequencing we saw earlier).

Input then must focus on content. It must be only roughly sequenced and in sufficient quantities that the "next level up" is assured to be present. It must also be somehow interesting and/or relevant to the acquirer, for reasons that will become clear in the following section. Most important, it must be comprehensible. The techniques for assuring that the acquirers, especially beginners, understand the input are much the same as those that parents have always used to make sure that young children understand their message: short, simple sentences with relatively simple vocabulary, lots of repetition, long pauses, explanation of new words, and subject matter limited for the most part to the "here and now" (see Hatch 1979 for a detailed description of "caretaker speech").

The final claim of the hypothesis is an intriguing one: the best way to teach someone to speak (in fact, the only way, according to Krashen) is by providing them with comprehensible input. In other words, we do not teach speaking at all. Speech will follow understanding, much as a child begins to speak long after it has begun to understand the language being spoken to it. When speaking, after all, we use the same rules as when listening, but without the advantage the listener has of being able to ignore much of the redundancy built into the message. Comprehension is naturally prior to production, both in first and second language acquisition, so why not teach it first?

Again, the theory would turn practice upside-down. Yet there are strong arguments in favor of postponing speech production. One recent study lists several (Gary and Gary 1981a, 335ff.): (1) production leads to language interference, borrowing elements from the native language;

(2) production overloads the short-term memory (there is so much more to think about); (3) production creates anxiety, and anxiety reduces acquisition; (4) production is less efficient in the classroom (only one student can use the rules at a time); (5) listening is, by nature, more communicative (it is easier to have students listen to "real" messages than to figure out how to have them produce them); (6) listening exercises are more adaptable to available media such as the language lab; and (7) listening is easier for a student to practice alone than is speaking. Chapter 3 will consider teaching methods that deliberately delay speech production for just these reasons.

2.5 THE AFFECTIVE FILTER HYPOTHESIS

The input hypothesis claims, in its simplest formulation, that if the LAD receives comprehensible input, acquisition will take place. Of course people are not machines, and it cannot be quite that simple. Whether acquisition is achieved or not will depend to a large extent on how the acquirer feels about what is taking place. To account for this, Dulay and Burt (1977) have proposed the notion of what is now called the Affective Filter: input will be "filtered" through the student's attitudes toward what is going on (motivation, self-confidence, anxiety); those with negative attitudes will have a "strong" filter, a sort of "mental block," that will prevent the input from reaching the LAD, and acquisition will not take place.

In a sense, this is nothing new. We have known for some time that success in language acquisition depended to a large extent on the acquirer's attitude. What the filter hypothesis gives us is a metaphor to suggest how this happens. Although the details of the filter and its operation may be somewhat vague, the implications for the teacher are clear enough. Above all, we should try to achieve a low-anxiety situation in the classroom. Much of that will come about simply because of the teacher's perceived attitude and body language and the "good vibes" that they generate in the classroom. We must try to avoid, says Stevick, letting our manner convey the unspoken message, "Now let's see if you can give a sensible answer to this one without making any mistakes" (1982, 122). Anxiety will be lessened also by activities that involve the students personally in such a way that they feel comfortable discussing themselves and their feelings and become genuinely interested in the feelings and opinions of the others. The material the teacher chooses can also make the students feel more at ease, because it is interesting, appropriate, and not frustratingly difficult.

But perhaps the two most important methods of reducing anxiety are suggested by the input model itself. First, the model claims that error correction is of little use in acquisition activities and should be restricted to learning activities. Much of the incentive for constant evaluation is gone, and along with it, much of the tension. Evaluation, whether praise or criticism, keeps the student "on the defensive," to use Stevick's term. Anxiety goes up, and performance goes down. Second, the model recommends delaying speaking until students have been exposed to enough comprehensible input that they feel ready to speak. This, too, relieves them of the often traumatic pressure to begin performing almost before they have a chance to understand anything in the new language. In retrospect, the classic audiolingual insistence not only on performance but on mistake-free performance from the first day must have been the source of a good number of more or less permanent "mental blocks."

2.6 SUMMARY: WHAT THE THEORY TELLS US

The input theory tells us that classroom activities should be directed more toward the unconscious acquisition of language than the conscious learning of rules. Acquisition will take place if we provide our students with sufficient quantities of comprehensible input, language they can understand and which is at their level or just a bit beyond (Chomsky's "rich linguistic environment"). This material should not be grammatically sequenced in any precise way. Class time should not be used for either grammatical explanation or drilling, and there should be no correction of errors except when the focus is on form. We should provide a relaxed and supportive atmosphere for the students, and we should not obligate them to begin speaking before they are ready.

The theory we have described here is of course just that, a theory consisting of a set of hypotheses. Like any carefully researched scientific theory, it is consistent with all the facts now before us, and we would expect it to be equally consistent with any new data that are uncovered. However, the reader should keep in mind that, as the theory is tested out in practice, we may well discover evidence of its limitations. We should remain alert to such evidence and open to making adjustments in the model as needed.

Meanwhile, the input model provides us with the most coherent and comprehensive theory of language acquisition that has come forth to date, one that may considerably alter the way we think about our profession. It offers us a succinct definition of the effective language teacher, as "someone who can provide input and make it comprehensible in a low-anxiety situation" (Krashen 1982, 32). Perhaps this is what many of us have been doing all along; perhaps not. But certainly as a profession we need principles on which to base our practice.

Chapter 3 considers the question of practice. We will look at a number of approaches to language teaching, both old and new, that are consistent with the principles implicit in the Chomskyan view of language in Chapter 1 and the input theory of acquisition just discussed.

chapter

3

Practice: Communicative Approaches to Language Teaching

It is probably an oversimplification, but it may be useful to imagine two basic schools of thought on language teaching, whose respective slogans might be (1) "Accuracy Before Fluency," and (2) "Fluency Before Accuracy." The grammar-translation method, the audiolingual method, and the cognitive-code method, with their emphasis on getting the form right, are all clearly examples of the first school. What we are witnessing in the 1980s is a gradual yet definite shift toward the second approach. It is not one method, but several, lumped together under the umbrella term "communicative language teaching." In part, this movement is due to the linguistic theories of Noam Chomsky and the findings of second language acquisition research, both of which were discussed in the previous chapters. In part, of course, it is simply the result of dissatisfaction with earlier approaches, which clearly were not living up to the claims being made for them.

I will not here attempt a history of language teaching (see Kelley 1969 or Diller 1978 for a review of the subject). I will instead examine some of the new (and not-so-new) methods of the fluency-before-accuracy school, and try to extract from them the "active ingredients" that make them work. This may not give us a fool-proof recipe for effective language teaching, but it should bring us a lot closer to it. Before we go any further, a clarification of terms: following Anthony's classic distinction, I will assume that an "approach" is a set of principles or beliefs about language teaching, whereas a "method" is a set of techniques—what we actually do in the classroom—that are used together (see Stevick 1982, 203).

3.1 THE GOAL: COMMUNICATIVE COMPETENCE

The goal of communicative methods is "communicative competence," which goes beyond what Chomsky meant by "(linguistic) competence," since it includes the added requirement that the speaker know how to use the language appropriately in a social situation. Terrell offers a very complete definition:

> I use the term to mean that a student can understand the essential points of what a native speaker says to him in a real communicative situation and can respond in such a way that the native speaker interprets the response with little or no effort and without errors that are so distracting that they interfere with communication. (Terrell 1977, reprinted in Blair 1982, 161)

Note that the key words in this definition are "understand" and "respond"—nothing is said about knowing the rules. Note, furthermore, that Terrell is not insisting that the student respond correctly, that is, entirely without mistakes, but rather without the kinds of mistakes that will get in the way of communication. In short, fluency before accuracy.

Given this goal, certain methodological strategies will follow, others will not. "Meaningful practice" will be preferred to "mechanical practice"—the kind that "goes into their ears and out their mouths without disturbing anything in between" (Stevick 1982, 13). Students will spend more time saying what they want to say, what they somehow need to say given the situation, and less time saying silly or irrelevant things that the book or the teacher or the tape would have them say. "We want the language learner to use the language," says Harvey (1982, 205). "That's how he's going to learn to use it. But we have to be sure that he's really using it, not just appearing to use it." The teacher's task then becomes primarily one of constructing situations that lead to "real use."

3.2 COMMUNICATIVE METHODS, OLD AND NEW

As with most good ideas, communicative language teaching is not new, but gets rediscovered from time to time. The direct methods of Berlitz (nearly a hundred years old) and DeSauze (from the 1930s) have many communicative features: exclusive use of the target language in the classroom, inductive presentation of grammar (i.e., instead of formal explanations, students figure out the rules from the examples practiced), avoidance of mechanical pattern drills in favor of contextualized practice, and heavy use of question-and-answer practice (cf. Diller 1978).[1]

More recently, the language teaching profession has become increasingly curious about a number of innovative methods, methods that often differ dramatically from what the establishment is doing. It is revealing to note how many of these have independently arrived at principles consistent with the theory of acquisition outlined in Chapter 2.

3.2.1 TPR and Other Listening Comprehension Approaches

Asher's Total Physical Response (TPR) focuses on developing listening comprehension by means of physical responses to command forms. Asher claims that body movements increase retention because they involve the right side of the brain, normally not used in the more "intellectual" approaches to learning. Regardless of whether we accept his neurological explanation for TPR, the method has its merits. Everything the teacher says (or the students later say) is a command. These begin with simple instructions to the class such as "Stand up" and "Sit down," but they can become much more elaborate, such as "John, stand up and walk over next to the girl with dark hair who is holding the red book." The first months of instruction are 70 percent listening comprehension (responding to commands), 20 percent speaking (when students are ready, usually after about ten hours of class), and 10 percent reading and writing (Asher et al. 1974). Judging from the results of Asher's research, the method is very effective, although as Krashen (1982, 141) points out, its success may in fact be due more to its massive doses of comprehensible input than to the use of physical responses. The crucial element, according to Krashen, is the understanding of the commands; the response merely confirms understanding. On the other hand, it may turn out that TPR works primarily because physical activity releases tension and lowers anxiety.

TPR is but one of a number of methods that concentrate on listening, often lumped together as "the comprehension approach" (Winitz 1981). In another version, Norman and Judith Gary (1981b) experimented in Egypt with teaching English by a method that was 100 percent listening at the outset, later 50 percent listening, 30 percent reading, and relatively little writing or speaking. Instead of using physical responses, students would show they understood by making marks or writing words on worksheets in front of them, later by writing in complete sentences in response to questions. The essential element, again, would appear to be their understanding of the material they heard, rather than the form of the response.

3.2.2 The Silent Way

In sharp contrast with the comprehension approach, where the teacher (or tape) talks almost all the time, Gattegno's Silent Way has the teacher silent most of the time. Silence is used as a dramatic way of focusing attention on the language and what it means. The instructor never gives an oral model more than once. Like a mute guide, the teacher leads the students with color-coded phonetic charts and colored rods to discover and understand the language on their own. Following the teacher's gestures or charades, they begin to produce original sentences and correct their own mistakes. Note that the method does place considerable emphasis on producing the correct form, with a resultant increase in student anxiety, especially at the beginning. As instruction proceeds, students become more and more responsible for their own learning, while the teacher says less and less. The goal is nothing less than independence in the new language (Gattegno 1976; Stevick 1970, 37–82).

3.2.3 Community Language Learning

Curran's Community Language Learning (CLL) is not strictly speaking a direct method since it makes heavy use of the native language. But it is overwhelmingly communicative: its principal strategy is simply to have students say whatever they want to. Students (or "clients") sit in a small circle with teachers (or "counselors") on the outside. At first the student gives her[2] message in her own language and the counselor, a "warm, sympathetic bilingual person," tells her how to say it in the target language. The student then repeats the message in the new language. Errors are not corrected at this point. Later the group will play back a tape of part of the conversation so that the counselor can write some of their original sentences on the board and talk about their structure. Curran emphasizes the importance of total trust and commitment between learners and counselors. The goal is self-confidence and, once again, independence in the new language (Curran 1972; Stevick 1980, 85–226).

3.2.4 Suggestology

Like Curran, Lozanov emphasizes the psychological environment for learning in his Suggestology or Suggestopedia method. The setting is crucial: sofas, soft lighting, classical music. The point, of course, is mental relaxation. Lozanov claims this leads to what he calls "hypermnesia"— greatly increased powers of memory. The basic strategy of the method is the "concert," the presentation of very long dialogs (at least ten pages) under these anxiety-free conditions, accompanied by music. (One demonstration Spanish class I observed used a Beethoven piano concerto for the first reading, read with somewhat exaggerated and dramatic intonation, and Vivaldi for the second, normal, reading.) Dialogs are designed to be both understandable and interesting to the student—clearly a good example of Krashen's "comprehensible input" in large doses. But Lozanov's success would appear to be largely due to his focus on reducing anxiety, on achieving a "low affective filter level," to use Krashen's term. Because of this basic strategy of delivering input under low-anxiety conditions, Suggestology comes very close to meeting the requirements of the Input Model. (For a detailed discussion of the method, see Stevick 1980, 229–59).

3.2.5 The Natural Approach

The method that most closely follows the outline of the Input Model of second language acquisition is Terrell's Natural Approach. It is a conscious attempt at producing acquisition rather than learning, i.e., the ability to use grammar rules rather than a conscious understanding of those rules. (Some grammatical explanation is provided, but as homework, not in the classroom.) The approach has three stages: (1) a prespeaking stage, with emphasis on listening comprehension by means of comprehensible input; techniques in this stage include TPR, extensive description of pictures, and a considerable amount of "teacher talk" about the classroom and its occupants, to which students need only respond with one-word answers to show understanding; (2) early speech production, which occurs when the students can recognize about 500 words and now feel confident about producing them, although still only in one- or two-word answers ("What color is this blouse? Blue."); and (3) the speech emergence stage, which uses games and activities that involve real communication, with focus always on the content rather than on the form. These include problem-solving activities such as completing together, as a class, a chart of the daily activities of the students. Rather than correct errors directly, which would call attention to form, the teacher tries to reconstruct or expand what the student has said, or simply model a better way of saying it (Terrell 1982).[3]

3.3 THE COMMON DENOMINATOR

Although they share a common goal (i.e., communicative competence), the methods just described obviously differ widely in their overall strategies. In fact, some of them, such as the Silent Way and Suggestology, would seem to be pulling in opposite directions (cf. Stevick 1980, 263–6). Yet there are certain features that most of these methods have in common, or that appear often enough to be worthy of mention: (1) meaningful rather than mechanical practice, (2) priority of listening over speaking, (3) exclusive use of the target language (except, as noted, in Community Language

Learning and the first part of a Suggestopedic lesson), (4) implicit rather than explicit grammar, (5) modeling instead of correction, and (6) special efforts to create a low-anxiety atmosphere in the classroom. (The Silent Way is the one exception to this list since it does not share features (2), (5), or (6).) Let us consider what each of these means in practice.

3.3.1 Meaningful Practice

"Meaningful" is used here in two senses: affective meaning (how much do the students care about what they are saying?), and cognitive meaning (how much sense does it make?). Students care about what they are saying if it is somehow about them or their life: daily activities, home, school, language class, plans, worries, etc. Wolfe (1967, 185) claims that "the amount of repetition required to learn a linguistic unit is reduced proportionally according to the intensity of the emotion involved in the repetition." For example, the Natural Approach and CLL both make a deliberate effort to have students talk about themselves, their feelings, their opinions.

The other sense of "meaningful" refers to the logic or truth value of what is being said. Unless deliberately false for effect (as in role-playing), each sentence should be a true, sensible statement, and somehow related to the sentences around it. We are far too accustomed to "lying" in the language class. We say the book is on the table when it isn't; we say John went to the movies last night when he didn't. And non sequiturs abound. In an exercise for practicing the use of the indirect object pronoun *le* in Spanish, one textbook would have American college students, presumably nowhere near a farm, utter things like "Le traemos las patatas esta tarde" ("We'll bring [him] the potatoes this afternoon") in one breath, then "¿Le enseño las ovejas el próximo invierno?" ("Shall I show [him] the sheep next winter?") in the next (Bolinger et al. 1966, 186). Such a haphazard collection of sentences, warned DeSauze, will "create in the mind of the student the distinct impression that the new language . . . only serves to illustrate grammatical relationship (DeSauze 1931, 10).

What *do* we talk about? About real things, about the "here and now." The Silent Way spends much of the time talking about the colored rods, pictures, and other realia in front of the students. TPR has students use the imperative to get other students to perform "here and now" actions— actions that often involve looking at, touching, or moving toward objects in the classroom. The Natural Approach emphasizes topics that are of personal interest to students: "Suppose you are a famous person, and there is a newspaper article about you. Tell at least one thing about yourself that is mentioned in that article . . ." (Krashen 1982, 138). In Suggestology students talk about the passage in front of them, or rework the material in games or skits. Talking can even be about grammar, because grammar is part of reality, and discussing it is practicing communication (Why do you say "une" and not "un"?, and so forth). But drilling is not talking, nor is repeating prefabricated dialogs or any other form of canned language. (For a detailed discussion of the kinds of activities that can serve as communicative practice, see Littlewood 1981.)

3.3.2 Listening Before Speaking

Krashen's Input Model (Chapter 2) claims that language acquisition occurs through exposure to "comprehensible input," massive doses of language we can understand, rather than through halting attempts at producing language that has not yet been assimilated. Early insistence on production creates unncessary tension and leads to overuse of the Monitor. Thus, the argument goes, speech should be delayed until the student has internalized enough of the rules that she feels confident about using them to generate her own sentences.

Several of the methods just described do just that. The various versions of the Comprehension Approach avoid speech for relatively long periods of time, if not most of the course, concentrating instead their efforts on developing strategies for listening and reading comprehension. TPR makes this possible by using physical responses instead of oral responses in the early stages. The prespeaking stage of the Natural Approach requires only a few one- or two-word answers to confirm understanding; in an earlier version (Terrell 1977), students were allowed to answer in their native language if they preferred—the response was felt to be less important than the act of understanding. The Suggestology "concert" amounts to a lengthy listening activity with no requirement to speak. All of these methods claim that delaying production not only lessens anxiety, but actually increases retention and—in some studies, at least—leads to better oral skills, even better pronunciation, when students eventually do begin speaking (Winitz and Reeds 1973).

3.3.3 Exclusive Use of the Target Language

If acquisition results from exposure to target-language input, there is obviously little value in using the native language in the classroom—for whatever purpose. Proponents of the classic direct methods (such as Berlitz) have long argued along these lines. Total elimination of the native language, says DeSauze (1931, 19), creates an authentic linguistic atmosphere and encourages both teacher and students to try to express themselves in the new language. Besides, he argues, once the teacher begins using the native language, the tendency is to gradually slip into it more and more often. And using the native language in the classroom gives the impression that the target language is only good for relatively artificial exercises, that when students have anything important to say, they can always go back to their own language. That is clearly not what we want to teach our students.

How does the teacher get around using the native language? By using simple statements at first, with as many cognates as possible. By pointing, drawing pictures on the board, charades, and especially by paraphrasing. The paraphrase, using words and structures the students already know, may often seem clumsy and time-consuming. But, argues Lenard (1970, 45), "time gained by speaking [the native language] is actually time lost," since each time we revert to it as a "shortcut" we are missing a chance to practice the students' ability to understand the target language, to provide more comprehensible input. Explaining in the new language is using it to communicate something real, and it reinforces the idea that the student can understand without translating. Besides, as Lenard points out, translations are very often misleading and incomplete: *un reloj* is more than either a clock or a watch, since it is both (ibid., 47).

3.3.4 Implicit Rather Than Explicit Grammar

Conscious attention to grammatical form, remember, leads only to "learning," not to acquisition; thus it can aid in the use of the Monitor, but not in production. The communicative methods we have seen generally regard grammar as little more than another bit of the real world to occasionally talk about when it comes up. The rules are of course there, embedded in the input. But in any listening-centered approach (including TPR), for example, they are acquired unconsciously. CLL seldom mentions grammar, Suggestology only in the introductory stage of each lesson. The Silent Way quietly models structure, or uses rods to represent structural elements. And the Natural Approach, although it does teach grammar as homework, emphasizes the importance of activities that *use* grammar: "Grammar rules are acquired over long periods of time, and proficiency with any particular grammar rule will occur only after considerable experience with real communication" (Terrell 1982, 126). The overt teaching of grammar is for the most part just that—teaching grammar, not language.

3.3.5 Modeling Instead of Correction

Terrell (1977, 1982) has been the most outspoken opponent of the overt correction of errors in the classroom: "The practice of correcting speech errors directly is not just merely useless, but actually harmful to progress in language acquisition" (1982, 126). He offers three reasons for avoiding direct correction: (1) it does not contribute to acquisition; (2) it creates a tense, evaluative atmosphere; and (3) it leads to focus on form, distracting from meaning-centered activities (ibid., 128). His Natural Approach does not, as we have seen, advocate simply ignoring errors, but rather finding ways to help students recognize their errors and eventually straighten them out by themselves. Written compositions are corrected, but there, too, the emphasis will be on improving the transmission of the message rather than on trying to achieve a native-like look to the sentences.

What is done in place of overt correction has come to be called "modeling." Mistakes that do not get in the way of understanding are usually ignored. The more serious mistakes are responded to either by asking questions intended to clarify the student's meaning, or by expanding the answer and then continuing the interchange:

Teacher:	What day is today?
Student:	Today Thursday.
Teacher:	Right, today is Thursday.
	So what day is tomorrow, then?

Community Language Learning and Suggestology either employ this modeling approach or treat mistakes as one more "real" thing to talk about. In the Silent Way, on the other hand, the teacher usually gives a subtle hand signal to indicate that a mistake has been made, or perhaps points to the rod that shows where it occurred; this is, note, actually a form of correction.

3.3.6 Low-Anxiety Atmosphere

Lozanov's experiments have shown that as students' fears are broken down, the resultant lack of inhibition stimulates both their memory and their fluency. The Affective Filter Hypothesis (Chapter 2) offers one explanation why this is so. Although we may not use sofas and classical music, there is much we can do to ease tension. Specific techniques depend on the age and interests of the group, but each of the methods just described offers insight into the process: avoiding evaluation, avoiding "putting the student on the spot"; not forcing production before the student is ready; encouraging the student to enter into a sense of play, of fictitious creativity. Lozanov suggests assigning students fictitious personalities to use in the classroom as a kind of mask to hide behind. Curran recommends the opposite: let the students be themselves and enjoy the therapeutic benefits of opening up to the others. Above all, the teacher must be supportive—never intimidating.

3.4 RESEARCH IN APPLIED LINGUISTICS: A FOOTNOTE

There have been a number of classic studies comparing this method and that method. I will not go into the details here; see Chastain 1976 and Diller 1978 for a discussion both of the studies and the problems inherent in carrying them out. What is curious about studies that compare traditional methods such as audiolingual and cognitive-code is that they never seem to uncover any significant differences in results. Yet, says Stevick (1976, 104), this is a contradiction:

> In the field of language teaching, Method A is the logical contradiction of Method B: if the assumptions from which A claims to be derived are correct, then B cannot work, and vice-versa. Yet one colleague is getting excellent results with A and another is getting excellent results with B. How is this possible?

One explanation is that traditional methods show similar results because they are all erroneously aimed at learning rather than acquisition (Krashen 1982, 154). Students will "learn" equally well with any of these methods, but they will not acquire language, except incidentally.

Recent studies comparing the newer communicative methods and the traditional methods, although still far from comprehensive, are more promising. Not surprisingly, methods aimed at acquisition fare better than those aimed more at learning in any measure of communicative skills. (See Krashen 1982, 155–60, and Krashen and Terrell 1983, for a review of some of these studies.)

3.5 SUMMARY: IS THERE A PERFECT METHOD?

Faced with a somewhat motley and confusing assortment of methods and the still inconclusive evidence of comparative studies, the response of many teachers, and of many of those writing on language teaching, has been simply to declare themselves "eclectics," "to choose parts of each system in the belief that the answer must be somewhere in the middle" (Krashen 1982, 154). Foreign language teaching in 1980, at least in the colleges, consisted for the most part of a "modified audiolingual approach," according to one survey—"modified" in the sense that increasing amounts of meaningful practice are finding their way into the classic dialog-and-drill format (Benseler and Schulz 1980, 93). So there is a movement of sorts. But it is far from organized, and terribly lacking in guidance: "We have no significant evidence that would enable us to recommend any one method-ological approach to foreign language teaching over another" (ibid., 94).

Need we be so cautious? The fact is, we do have evidence and we can make recommendations. As we saw in Chapter 1, Chomsky gives us a powerful model of the richness and complexity of language that compels us to abandon any notions of learning by mere conditioning or analogy, and that calls on the teacher to create a "rich linguistic environment" in which language can grow. Krashen (Chapter 2) suggests what this environment might consist of—"rich" in comprehensible input delivered under low-anxiety conditions—and his distinction between learning and acquisition would lead us to discard the bulk of our structure-centered classroom practices. Finally, we have experimental evidence, innovative methods that have devised ingenious ways of creating a "rich linguistic environment," many of them focusing on comprehensible input. Although we might never actually use any of these methods exclusively in the classroom, we can learn from them and be changed by them.

Is there a recipe for a perfect method? Probably not. In the end, of course, we all end up using our own, because language teaching is very personal and we are all different. But it need not be the tossed salad of unprincipled eclecticism (where we often end up choosing the wrong things for the wrong reasons), but rather a carefully blended soufflé made with the best and most promising ingredients available—with the reassuring knowledge that those ingredients have a sound theoretical and experimental basis.

NOTES TO CHAPTER 3

1. There is currently somewhat of a revival of interest in DeSauze's method, particularly in the teaching of French; see especially Lenard 1970 and Hester 1970.

2. Since I teach in a women's college, I will throughout refer to students with feminine pronouns.

3. For more detailed information on the Natural Approach, see Krashen and Terrell 1983.

PART
two

Computers and Language Teaching

At no previous time has it been possible to create learning resources so responsive and interesting, or to give such free play to the student's initiative as we may now. (Nelson 1970)

chapter

4

The Language Lab Analogy: Uses and Misuses of Technology

The language teaching profession has always shown a curious weakness for leaping on bandwagons, whether they involved the very latest and most "scientific" teaching method or simply the newest technological gadget. Listen to a few typical claims for the latest electronic aid:

"This technology will revolutionize the teaching of foreign languages; it will bring pedagogy up to date with technology."

"Finally we have a means for true individualized practice: one-on-one, self-paced, without need for supervision. Students can practice what they want, whenever they want, for as long as they want."

"These devices will do all the things the teacher has neither the time nor the inclination to do; at last we can take drill out of the classroom."

That was twenty years ago, when the latest fad was the audio language lab, not the computer. But note the remarkable similarity in the claims being made today for computer-assisted language instruction. So strong is the sensation of *déjà vu* that it would probably be instructive to reflect on the language lab experience to see if there is not a lesson in there someplace.

4.1 A BRIEF HISTORY

Consider what took place in the late 1950s and early 1960s. Following the launching of sputnik in 1957, the language profession went into a crisis. Whatever we were doing was obviously inadequate. We needed new methods, new tricks. In the midst of this state of apprehension and self-criticism, the language lab manufacturers began touting their marvelous machines. The hardware was impressive, and great hopes were advanced: technology would save the foreign language profession. Schools everywhere rushed to buy the new machines, and a lot of money (including federal grants) was spent.

But once the hardware was installed, most schools did not seem to have a clear idea what it was for. Labs were "often mandated by administrators who themselves knew little or nothing about foreign language instruction but had been convinced by others that the machines were going to revolutionize foreign language instruction and produce near-native fluency in all students" (McCoy and Weible 1983, 110).[1] The manufacturers, meanwhile, had conveniently glossed over the software question, and it quickly became clear that good software was not easy to find. Commercially prepared tapes were more often than not of poor quality, or simply unsuitable for or irrelevant to classroom activities. Producing new tapes meant one more demand on teachers' time, with results of uneven quality in any case. Meanwhile the students quickly tired of the novelty, began to resent being forced to sit there with those uncomfortable earphones on, and started taking the booths apart.

Because of the way it ended up being used, the lab simply could not live up to its expectations. Although the hardware evolved through several increasingly sophisticated generations, the software did not keep pace. "Much language programming," says Rivers (1981, 425), "is still steeped in the theories of the fifties." Of course the original design was transparently behaviorist: it was a device for practicing pattern drills. The student, alone and isolated in her booth, was supposed to repeat and repeat until she had "overlearned" the patterns, and made them a matter of unconscious habit. The lab was seen as a sort of tireless teacher's aide that could drill the mechanical aspects of language, freeing the teacher for more creative activities. In fact, so closely was the lab bound to audiolingual practices, it probably had a lot to do with keeping the ALM alive for so long: even after behaviorist principles had been subjected to serious question, there was an understandable reluctance to discard the texts, tapes, and (especially) the expensive hardware that went with them.

Eventually, though, teachers began to suspect that the language lab was probably not doing that much good, and a number of studies that appeared at about that time largely confirmed their suspicions. The *coup de grâce,* perhaps, was the Pennsylvania Foreign Language Project (1965–69), a four-year study of language teaching methods that concluded, among other things, that "using the lab twice each week had no discernible effect on . . . achievement" (Smith 1970). In fact, the effect was often negative—an earlier study seemed to indicate that although the average student's progress was relatively unaffected by using the language lab, students with high IQ's were actually slowed down (Keating 1963). With or without studies, it was obvious that students were developing a strong distaste for language labs, a distaste that unfortunately carried over to language learning in general: "To some extent it is accurate to say that our profession has spent the last 15 years working to overcome the mindless embrace of what should have been a highly helpful instructional medium" (McCoy and Weible 1983, 133).

4.2 THE LANGUAGE LAB: LIMITATIONS

The classic audio language lab program involves both listening and speaking. Although the listening component may well be a meaningful exercise, rich in comprehensible input, speaking into a deaf machine is clearly of questionable value. Consider the drawbacks:

1. **The student must correct herself.**

   The idea was that each student would compare her own responses with the "correct" responses on the master track. But it just didn't work. Only a small percentage of students, says Hester (1970, 79), can even recognize their mistakes; even fewer can correct them. "There is reason to believe," conclude Epting and Bowen (1979, 75), "that most students do not benefit from listening to their own responses." The only solution was to monitor the lab, thereby defeating the purpose of providing outside practice on a flexible schedule.

2. **All utterances are prefabricated.**

   The student's answers are necessarily not original, since they have to agree with the master responses on the tape. There is thus no innovation, no creativity, and very little cognitive activity of any kind.

3. There is no semblance of communication.

The student is only too aware that she is talking to herself, and thus that she is not communicating anything. She is also aware that this is, therefore, not "real" language, only adding to her frustration. The problem becomes acute as the student advances and feels a growing need to respond to contextually meaningful utterances requiring a natural speaker-hearer exchange. "There is no question," concede Epting and Bown (ibid., 75), "that the language lab is ill-suited for presentation of highly communicative exercises."

4. The student is passive rather than active.

The effectiveness of a lab exercise, or a classroom activity, depends on how actively students are participating. "Active," we have seen, means mentally involved in the meaning of what is being said. A lab drill requiring nothing more than repetition is a passive exercise.

5. The program is inflexible.

Since the tape deck is deaf, it keeps going at the same speed with the same exercises regardless of what is taking place at the other end. The student has to muddle through even if she is in over her head. She has no control over the program except to stop it or start it, and she can only control the level of difficulty by asking for a different tape. And through it all there is no feedback to the student on how well she is doing, or whether or not she is wasting her time.

One example of such a lab exercise is sufficient to make the point. What follows is a portion of the lab exercise on SER and ESTAR in *Modern Spanish* (Bolinger et al. 1966). It is not by any means the worst of its kind, since the interchange has a certain naturalness to it (I shall forgo translation here on the assumption that the flavor is evident even when one does not understand all the details):

TAPE	STUDENT
¿Julio? ¿Enfermo?	Sí, Julio está enfermo.
¿La tía? ¿amable?	Sí, la tía es amable.
¿Susana? ¿de México?	Sí, Susana es de México.
¿Todos? ¿en casa?	Sí, todos están en casa.
¿Doña Mercedes? ¿bien?	Sí, doña Mercedes está bien.
¿La casa? ¿bonita?	Sí, la casa es bonita.
¿Julio? ¿en su cuarto?	Sí, Julio está en su cuarto.
etc.	

One advantage of this exercise over many lab drills is that the student would have to have some idea of what the sentences mean in order to answer correctly. Yet it is hardly communicative practice. The only motivation the student has for saying what she does is entirely external: the tape gives her a stimulus, she provides a response. And of course it is highly doubtful that the student will want to talk about "Julio" or "la tía" or "doña Mercedes" in the first place. The student would prefer to talk about herself or people she knows.

4.3 COMMUNICATIVE USES OF THE LANGUAGE LAB

In light of these obvious drawbacks, there is much talk about reappraising the language lab and trying to find ways to use it that are more appropriate both to lab design and our current emphasis on communicative practice. The lab's obvious strength is in the area of listening comprehension, where there is no pretense of two-way communication. The easiest and best use of the lab, says Krashen (1982, 185), is as a means of supplying "comprehensible input": taped stories with pictures, radio programs, commercials, and so forth. Hester (1970, 79) and Chastain (1976, 540) both suggest making greater use of listening exercises accompanied by written comprehension questions; likewise, all of the lab programs discussed in Epting and Bowen's paper (1979) are some sort of variation on this idea: taped lectures with written questions, "lecturettes" with cloze-type exercises and comprehension questions, and so forth—none of them involves oral student responses.

But the general consensus is not overly enthusiastic. For Chastain, the question of whether the audio lab can be adapted to communicative methods remains to be answered (ibid.). It is clear that the lab's weaknesses are serious ones. Can we justify maintaining all that expensive hardware just to allow our students to do an occasional listening exercise? Tracy Terrell (personal communication) points out that even for listening comprehension the lab is limited, since listening strategies involve not just monitoring sounds, but watching facial expressions and gestures, and interacting with the speaker for clarification. The solution, some say, is to use the lab as a true audiovisual or multi-media center, where students could watch slides or filmstrips while listening to cassettes. In some labs each booth has a small video monitor so that students can check out and review videotapes. With this combination of image and sound, the potential for providing comprehensible input is clearly enormous. So, unfortunately, are the costs.

4.4 THE COMPUTER VERSUS THE LANGUAGE LAB

The primary defect of the audio lab as it is currently conceived is that it cannot react to the student's response, i.e., it is incapable of feedback. It is not surprising, then, that there is growing interest in investigating the use of the interactive computer as a language teaching aid and possible supplement to or replacement for present language lab hardware. It is not hard to see why. Consider the drawbacks of the lab which we listed in Section 4.2. In the lab, the student must correct herself; the computer, on the other hand, can "read" the student's response and respond accordingly, with a comment or an explanation, or by merely pointing to her mistake. Sentences in the lab are all prefabricated; a computer program could allow the student to compose her own response, while composing some of its own. Whereas there is clearly no communication in the lab, in a sophisticated interactive program there could at least be the "feel" of communication. The student at the computer terminal need not be passive at all, especially if the program allows her to create her own responses. And, finally, the computer program could offer flexibility where the lab cannot, branching to different subprograms depending on how the student responds.

The now standardized term for the use of computers as an instructional tool is computer-assisted (sometimes "-aided") instruction (CAI); in language teaching there is increasing use of the term computer-assisted language instruction (CALI). The term "instruction" is somewhat misleading in both cases, though, since most CAI systems are used for drill and practice or review, and very seldom for actual instruction. For this reason I will here use the more recent term "computer-assisted language learning" or CALL.

Computer-assisted language learning, when compared to what it could be, has so far been a decidedly lackluster enterprise. There are a number of reasons for this. One is simply the newness of it all. Language teachers who have experimented with computers have generally not had a chance to become sophisticated programmers and have thus been unable to make very good use of the computer. On the other hand, the computer people who do have the expertise usually do not know enough about the language teaching business to come up with anything appropriate. And, at least until quite recently, educational software has not been a sufficiently viable commercial venture to merit the investment of expensive programming time. Now that publishing houses are getting into the act, the situation may change, although what the publishers have done so far is hardly impressive. Whatever the explanation, a survey of CALL work to date reveals an array of prosaic "drills" that have not, as far as one can tell from the literature, made any significant impact on the technology of foreign language teaching in our schools and colleges.

What is worse, we seem to be falling into the same pattern of failure that characterized our use of the language lab: mesmerized by the hardware, we remain remarkably uncritical of the software and its underlying principles. Once again we see the hardware companies pushing their equipment on the schools while skirting around the embarrassing lack of decent software. Again we see administrators purchasing technology they do not understand, encouraging teachers to use it in ways that go against their pedagogical principles or to use programs that are unrelated to their curricular goals. We see the students, first fascinated, later puzzled or frustrated because the programs make mistakes or simply do not make any sense. Again, the novelty will wear off—perhaps even faster this time. And if we do not have anything interesting or challenging to offer our students when it does, we are going to be stuck with another pile of expensive equipment gathering dust in a closet somewhere.

If there is a lesson to be learned from the language lab episode, it is that the success or failure of any technological aid will have less to do with what it *can* do than with what we actually end up doing with it. There is nothing particularly wrong with the audio lab once you recognize its limitations—the problem was the mindless way we went about using it. And it was clearly not simply the fault of the teachers. Under pressure to use the labs in whatever way they could, they turned to what was readily available and obvious.

History has this funny way of repeating itself. Teachers will soon be under pressure to find some use—any use—for all those Apples and TRS-80s. Most of them will not have the time to develop their own software (an extremely labor-intensive business), and they will turn to what is readily available and obvious. But perhaps it will turn out better this time if (1) programmers can be shown what it is we really need, and (2) we teachers can develop a strong critical sense for what is good and useful, and what is not, in educational software.

NOTE TO CHAPTER 4

1. References for Chapters 4 through 8, except those cited previously in earlier chapters, will be found in References, Part Two.

chapter

5

CALL: The State of the Art

I am using the phrase "state of the art" somewhat ironically here, since computer-assisted language learning (CALL) is far from being a recognizable, coherent "art," and its "state" is, at best, highly tentative. As has been pointed out, "Computer-Assisted Instruction sounds like something exact and impressive, but is in fact a scattering of techniques tied together only nominally by a general idea" (Nelson 1974, 15). Of course, things are changing fast. Computer literacy is clearly on the increase, among both teachers and students. An impressive amount of hardware is available for "hands-on" experimentation (the average U.S. high school had 11 microcomputers in 1983). There is even a certain amount of software on the market now—some 100 foreign language programs in one recent survey (Harrison 1983). Yet we are still groping in the dark, grasping at the first and most obvious ideas that come along. We now have access to some of the most complex and sophisticated technology around, machines that can perform millions of operations per second and complete the most intricate logical operations, and we can think of nothing better to do with them than the most primitive and trivial sort of fill-in-the-blank exercises.

Our profession of course has a history of misusing or failing to understand new technology; witness our hapless romance with the language lab, documented in the last chapter. It might be instructive to review here how the language profession first began experimenting with computers.

5.1 CALL: EARLY EXPERIMENTS

It may come as a surprise to some that computer-assisted language learning has been going on in some form since the 1960s. In those early days, before the proliferation of microcomputers, experiments with computers and language instruction were almost exclusively confined to college language departments with access to the college's mainframe (i.e., non-micro) computer system. Working with a large system, early experimenters tended to think big. Some felt that a complete CAI system might well provide an alternative to classroom instruction, rather than merely a supplement, as in the current view. One problem with all these systems from the outsider's point of view was that we almost never had a chance to try them out. Usually developed for use on one particular set of hardware, they were seldom transportable in anything resembling the way in which floppy disks can now be mailed from one micro user to another. This means that most of what we know about these experiments is what can be gleaned second-hand from the literature.

One of the first projects involved the development of special CAI terminals and programmed materials at IBM (Rosenbaum 1969) for the teaching of beginning German at the State University of New York at Stony Brook. In addition to grammar exercises (which incorporated graphic answer-processing strategies similar to DASHER—see below), the system allowed for listening comprehension, vocal practice, dictation, and translation exercises. The Stony Brook project was unique in that it involved experimenting with a fully computerized German section and comparing the results with conventional instruction; results were initially favorable, if somewhat inconclusive (Adams et al. 1968; Morrison and Adams 1968).

Certainly the most ambitious CALL project is the one that has been running on the PLATO system, developed at the University of Illinois/ Urbana and now marketed by the Control Data Corporation. PLATO, again, is a totally instructional system: the basic design, the programming language (TUTOR), the programs, even the terminals, were all developed exclusively for CAI. Programs have been written, mostly by teachers, for French, Spanish, German, ESL, Latin, Russian, Chinese, and Hebrew. After several years of experimentation, the University of Illinois continues to offer language sections in which part of the work will be done on PLATO. (See Hart 1981 for an overview of PLATO; other articles in this special issue of *Studies in Language Learning* provide detailed information on PLATO programs.)[1]

Other examples of mainframe systems include:

— Dartmouth's CARLOS (Computer-Assisted Review Lessons on Syntax) provided second-year students with homework exercises in Spanish, French, and Danish (Turner 1970; Allen 1972).

— A program in reading scientific German at MIT allowed users to ask questions about the meaning and structure of the sentences while translating (Nelson et al. 1976).

— A sizeable Spanish program at the University of Minnesota/Duluth running on a system known as CALLS (Computer-Assisted Language Learning System) was flexible enough in design that beginning and advanced students could use the same program by merely requesting the topic and level they wished to work on (Boyle 1976).

Many of these mainframe efforts showed a certain amount of sophistication in programming techniques. Allen's French program at Dartmouth, for example, edited student input so that the computer could discriminate between significant and nonsignificant errors (typos, extra letters, etc., were just ignored) and could judge significant errors as "close" or "not close"—if close, students got a second chance to answer. And if students decided at any point that what they were doing was too easy, they could request to skip to harder material (Allen 1972; Allen 1971 gives a listing of the BASIC subroutines that edit student input).

Others experimented with "generative" programs, which used a set of rules to generate new linguistic content, rather than relying on a prefabricated stock of sentences. ZAP, a French program at the University of California, Riverside, used its generative rules in a slightly different way. The student would make up the sentences and then have the program perform grammatical operations on them—negation, questions, change of subject, etc. These operations could be used for illustration (computer performs them), drill (both student and computer perform, and results are compared), or testing (same as drill, except that the student's success or failure is counted). The rules were sufficiently generalized that the program could perform these operations on any initial string. (Decker 1976; ZAP is about to be published as part of a French software package, VERBSTAR).

5.2 THE MICRO AGE

Enter the Apple (and PET and TRS-80, and so forth). Overnight, language teachers at all levels are either trying their hand at programming or looking frantically for software. It has quickly become clear that good, intelligent software is neither simple to write nor easy to find. Commercially available programs are usually written by computer experts with no training in language pedagogy, whereas the efforts of language teachers—although perhaps pedagogically sound—are usually woefully unsophisticated uses of the computer. "Even as computer literacy increases," says Putnam (1983) in a very sensible review of the CALL software problem, "equal expertise in foreign-language pedagogy and computers is rare and likely to remain so."

As of this writing there have been two extensive reviews of software available for foreign language practice. One is Harrison's article in the *NECTFL Newsletter* (Harrison 1983). The author lists over 100 programs available at that time for the Apple II, most of which came on the market in the latter part of 1982. Of these, he rates 14 "of very high quality and usefulness" and 5 "an essential purchase." Harrison's overall judgment is guarded: the industry, he concludes, is "still in a state of infancy" (ibid., 30).

The other major review is actually a collection of reviews, the report of the software evaluations done by a group of teachers at a summer institute on CALL in 1982 (Culley and Mulford 1983). After reviewing some 25 language programs, the consensus was less than enthusiastic; the participants went home, say the authors, "generally dissatisfied" with the software available and convinced that it did not exploit the potential for micro-aided instruction. Some comments taken from their reviews of specific programs (page numbers in parentheses):

"There is almost no interaction [with] the student." (1)

"Far too many editing errors . . . too frustrating." (3)

"Little is done here that flashcards could not do." (7)

"If an error of any kind is made, the student is immediately provided with the correct answer without an opportunity to try again." (12)

"The only way it provides for individualization is by the student's choice to replay a whole section of the lesson." (19)

"From the standpoint of instructional design, the programs for all their fancy graphics and audio are strangely primitive." (28)

To help us understand their dissatisfaction, let us take a closer look at a Spanish program to which they gave relatively high marks and which in many ways typifies the current software market.

The program is called PRACTICANDO ESPANOL CON LA MANZANA II (Phillips 1981). It consists of two parts, verb conjugation drills and vocabulary translation drills. The verb drills cover all indicative tenses, present and past subjunctive, plus command forms. A typical interchange looks like this:

```
(ELLA Y E'L) VIVIR

---->  vivimos

NO, WRONG.  PLEASE TRY AGAIN

---->  vivi's

STILL WRONG, SUSIE.

  >>   THE RIGHT ANSWER IS:  VIVEN

       REGULAR.  FORM ENDS IN EN

NOW PLEASE TYPE THE CORRECT ANSWER

---->
```

What the reviewers apparently liked about this program is that it offers a certain amount of interactive help. The student may type "help" for a hint, "review" for explanation and/or verb-ending chart, "answer" for the answer, "change" to go to a different drill, or "stop" to end the drill. It apparently runs without glitches, is easy to use, and has a well-written manual. The reviewers also appreciated the program's friendly tone ("I will give you two chances and then I will tell you the answer"). Yet it is not hard to imagine why they went home dissatisfied. For all its technical excellence and lack of glitches, PRACTICANDO is just one more drill-and-practice exercise, a workbook sheet with feedback. It is not, by any stretch of the imagination, "meaningful practice." It was gratifying to see this defect pointed out in a separate review published elsewhere (Meredith 1981). Although Meredith's comments are largely favorable, he finds the program somewhat mechanical. "Perhaps the most significant improvement," he says "would be to require the student to understand the *meaning* [my emphasis] of the Spanish item in order to complete it correctly."

One programmer has taken a step in that direction. Schaeffer (1981) describes an experiment in which he compares the effectiveness of mere structural drill (as in PRACTICANDO) with that of what he somewhat erroneously labels "semantic drill"—actually structural drill with some semantic content. The difference in the latter is that the student, before coming up with the correct verb ending, must first choose the appropriate verb to fit the content of the sentence. He gives the following example (ibid., 134):

```
Structural drill

    Instructions:  Provide the correct form of the verb
    "haben" and the past participle of the verb in
    parentheses.

        Wir _____ den Mann _____ (suchen)

        Auf wen _____ Sie _____ ? (warten)

Semantic drill

    Instructions:  Select the appropriate verb for each
    sentence from the infinitives below.  Type the
    corresponding past participle in the space provided.

        Verbs:  glauben, machen, rauchen, regnen

        Ich habe die Geschichte _____ .

        Es hat die ganze Nacht _____ .
```

This is arguably an improvement over a purely structural drill which can be completed entirely without having any idea what the words mean. Yet the "context" does not go beyond that of each sentence, and the sentences are entirely unrelated one to the other. There is still no communication in any real sense.

5.3 THE "WRONG-TRY-AGAIN" MODEL

What is clearly missing from the vast majority of CALL programs is anything resembling what we do when we use language, any semblance of communication, even so much as the "feel" of conversation. They do not exploit the power of the computer to interact in an intelligent way with the user. They do not exploit the inherent flexibility of the computer, which can read and respond to a wide range of possible student answers. Nor do they allow the student to do anything creative, to say what she wants to say rather than what the program wants her to say.

One of the explanations for this is that underlying most of these programs is a largely unspoken assumption about what CALL *is* and what it is for. Says Hart (1981, 12) about the language teachers who developed the PLATO materials "most . . . have concluded that PLATO is best used to implement the more mechanical types of vocabulary and grammar drill, thereby freeing teachers for more expressive activities." In other words, it is assumed that CALL is a computerized form of programmed instruction (PI), whereby the material is broken down into a series of clearly defined steps or "frames," each of which supposedly can be easily learned. "Tutorial computer use," says Levien (1972, 377), "is directly descended from the teaching machines of the type pioneered by B. F. Skinner." Creating these frames in turn means breaking the language itself down into bite-sized chunks—discrete points of grammar or vocabulary, mostly out of context and devoid of any real meaning. The result: grammar fill-ins and vocabulary translation exercises, often called "flashcard programs." It is ironic that at the same time our profession was discovering communicative methodology, which discouraged piecemeal morphological drill in favor of global practice, the CALL people were busy cutting language up into largely meaningless little pieces.

From a pedagogical point of view, there are three principal defects in programs of the PI type, or what I prefer to call the "wrong-try-again" model: (1) they focus on form rather than meaning (hence contribute mostly to learning rather than to acquisition); (2) what little help or feedback they do give with form is often sketchy or vague; and, most important, (3) they assume that the computer should be an evaluative taskmaster that asks all the questions and judges all the answers. Let us consider each of these defects in detail.

5.3.1 Focus on Form

When Pusack writes that "foreign languages are by nature an area where computer-assisted instruction should thrive," he is thinking of pattern practice: "Students need extensive practice in applying the rules of the new language. This routine process involves predictable patterns of right and wrong answers, and thus is a natural application for computers" (Pusack 1981, 5). "Natural" is used here only in the sense of "obvious." It is also perfectly "natural" for a computer to perform a million operations a second, somewhat more than the number needed to decide if *quiero* is spelled right or not. Pusack goes on to argue that drill is really all computers can do, since they cannot understand what sentences mean, hence "student-initiated questions and free-form answers lie outside the capability of today's machines and programs, except in highly restricted contexts" (ibid.). Yet note that this last statement implies, quite rightly, that within restricted contexts computers should in fact be capable of "understanding" answers that go beyond "predictable patterns of right and wrong answers." In Chapter 7 we will look at "intelligent" programs that in fact do just that.

In arguing, however, that "true understanding" is beyond the scope of computers, the pessimists somewhat miss the point. The choice is not simply between mechanical drill at one extreme and human-like simulated intelligence at the other. For a computer program to be capable of meaningful interchange with the user, it does not have to understand at anything approaching the level of human understanding (which is indeed beyond its capability). Clearly there are many in-between levels of partial understanding, what we might call "semi-intelligent systems," that can be extremely useful as interactive instructional aids. Then, too, linguistic material can be made more meaningful to the system user in many ways. We will look at examples of both these approaches in Chapters 6 and 7.

5.3.2 The Feedback Problem

Even allowing that learning-oriented practice with grammatical form might be useful under some circumstances, and that we would like to see programs that help students with grammar, the problem of feedback remains. Pusack (1983a) provides a useful typology of answer-processing strategies. Right answers, as he points out, are no problem; things only get interesting when the student makes a mistake. There are basically five ways of dealing with the problem. The first is simply not to evaluate at all; in Chapter 6 we will look at some "communicative" programs that use this approach.

The second strategy is the most common, namely to judge the answer as either right or wrong. In some cases, there is no hint as to what the problem is. After two (maybe three) wrong tries, the computer simply gives you the answer. Complained one student of just such a program, "It just blurts out what has to be said, and if you don't know it, it doesn't help you" (Terry 1977, 197). Other programs use "partial answer processing" to try to diagnose the error. As we will see in Chapter 8, this can be very complicated to do.

An entirely different approach to error handling is what is known as "pattern markup." Here the student's input is treated as a meaningless string of characters to be matched against the "correct" answer; any discrepancy in the student's response is marked. Students thus get a visual, rather than verbal, judgment on what they have written. The typical PLATO program accomplishes this by means of TUTOR's built-in error-marking functions. The same principle is used in DASHER (Pusack 1983b) as in this French drill where the student is supposed to change singulars to plurals:

```
COMPUTER:    La jeune fille est belle.  (pluriel)

Student:     La jeune filles est belle.
```

```
COMPUTER:    (Non.)

             L--- jeune- filles ----- belle-.
```

Other symbols are used to signal extra or transposed letters or words. Note that the computer is still saying "right" or "wrong," although now it can specify "wrong in this position" or "something should go here." It does not explain what the problem is (in terms of grammar rather than position), and it has no way of distinguishing between inflection errors, spelling errors, or typos.

The fourth strategy involves comparing the student's response with a list of possible wrong answers; this is known as "error anticipation." The better programs of this type try to use this diagnosis to provide hints of one sort or another as to the nature of the problem. In tutorial programs, these hints can be fairly specific, as in this German imperative program in use at Ohio State (Hope et al. 1984, 46):

```
COMPUTER:    Herr Klein, --------- die Rechnung!
             (bezahlen)

Student:     bezahlen

COMPUTER:    You forgot an important part of the polite
             imperative. Try again and remember to
             include the missing part.
```

The final strategy in Pusack's list is parsing. Here the program, instead of containing the "correct" pattern to be matched, or a list of anticipated errors, will have some built-in strategy for analyzing the student's response and detecting the presence of anomalies. This would enable considerably greater flexibility in the kind of response the student could give and in the form of the feedback. Such strategies come under the heading of "artificial intelligence," which we will consider at some length in Chapter 7.

5.3.3 The Computer as Taskmaster

Quite apart from its deficient analysis of grammar errors and its insensitivity to meaning, CALL of the "wrong-try-again" type suffers from a misconceived notion of the role of the computer. The computer, in this view, is a sort of taskmaster or quizmaster that asks all the questions, judges the student as good or bad, and makes all the decisions as to what is going to happen next.

This is, it turns out, the traditional view of CAI. In a seminal article published in the *Scientific American* in 1966, Stanford professor Patrick

Suppes outlined the basic principles of computer-assisted instruction as he saw them. His definition is classic CAI of the "wrong-try-again" type: the system will always decide what the student is going to study and will control her movements through it. Material will be presented in little chunks called frames, and student responses will be evaluated. The complexity of the system derives precisely from the problem of how it is to decide, at every step, where the student should go next, and how to evaluate the student's responses in a foolproof fashion.

As we have seen, these are still the principal concerns in the CALL literature: branching and answer-processing. Yet the crucial flaw in this approach is that it tries to simulate what the teacher does in the classroom—to be exact, the least interesting things the teacher does in the classroom ("simulate classroom drill," says Pusack), and thus free the teacher for more "creative" activities. As should have been clear from the discussion in Chapter 2, there are a good many problems with what goes on in the language classroom. It tends to be authoritarian, with the teacher controlling both the material and the form of presentation. It tends to be evaluative, with the student constantly being judged for rightness and wrongness (which in turn creates tension and anxiety). And it tends to be overly structured, everything carefully sequenced ("the structure of the day") and presented piece-by-piece in a way that can then later be "measured" and "evaluated." All of these drawbacks of the classroom tend to get in the way of language acquisition; many of the methods we looked at in Chapter 2 are specifically designed to avoid them or alleviate them. Yet the "classic" form of CALL re-creates precisely those features of the classroom we are trying to avoid: it is teacher- (i.e., computer-) controlled, evaluative, and highly structured.

It is a curious aspect of human nature that when we face something that is new to us, we try to make it seem familiar, like a tourist in a foreign country desperately looking for signs of home. So, too, with computers in education. The computer is a radically new medium, and yet we are clearly trying to use it in the old, familiar ways. We envision the student drilling away with the computer, one on one, when it may very well turn out that the best use we can make of the machine is to let it stimulate group activity. We try to design our programs so that all our students will be guided toward the same "correct" results, when perhaps the greatest advantage of this medium is precisely that it can allow the individual student to decide how the lesson should proceed. It may be, in fact, that what the computer is best at has nothing at all to do with what we do in the classroom. Perhaps, as some suggest, the real advantage of the computer is that it challenges us to use our brains to explore language, to play with it, to find out how it works and how it doesn't, "to replace 'You're wrong' with 'I win' " (Higgins and Johns 1984, 46).

5.4 SUMMARY: SOME ASSUMPTIONS ABOUT CALL

Perhaps one of the reasons so few programs have tried to break away from the "wrong-try-again" approach is that the literature is so full of pessimism regarding what computers can do: "The computer cannot initiate, or evaluate, communicative activities . . . The computer can [only] contribute to achieving linguistic competence, and the more advanced skills can be reserved for the classroom situation" (Odendaal 1982, quoted in Higgins 1983a, 104). Said an earlier pessimist, "CAI . . . is nothing more nor less than an analog of programmed instruction" and "provides too artificial a situation for conversational interaction" (Ornstein 1970, 216–217). In short, computers are best suited to leading students step by step, frame by frame, through the subject matter.

It is important to stress here that this negative view by no means reflects limitations in computers themselves, but rather limitations in the programs currently being written (or as Higgins suggests, "limitations in the imagination of the program writers" (ibid.)). Although much of the literature is devoted to arguing that the computer cannot do this or cannot do that, what is meant is that no one is doing it. Apparently, early experimenters assumed that CALL could be adapted most easily to the PI model, and those who came later for the most part imitated them. However, says Higgins, this need not be the case: "Programmed [instruction] certainly does impoverish acquisition, but the computer can be turned into a device which provides elements of caretaker speech [cf. Chapter 2] and a focus on meaning rather than form" (ibid.). In Chapter 6 we will explore ways in which this might be done.

NOTE TO CHAPTER 5

1. Control Data now markets PLATO materials for micros. For all the time and money that has been spent on the PLATO system, what is available to the micro user is for the most part a disappointingly primitive set of grammar drills and vocabulary games.

chapter

6

The Computer as a Communicative Environment

What are the alternatives to the approach documented in Chapter 5? What if people like Suppes had never "defined" CAI for us, and we had never seen examples of the "wrong-try-again" model? Recalling the principles of communicative language teaching from Part One, plus a little common sense, let us imagine how computers might be used in language teaching.

6.1 PREMISES FOR "COMMUNICATIVE" CALL[1]

1. Communicative CALL will aim at acquisition practice rather than learning practice. This means that the activities will focus more on using forms to communicate than on the forms themselves. There will be no drill.

2. In a Communicative CALL lesson or activity, grammar will always be implicit rather than explicit. Grammar will be built into the lesson. Grammatical explanation may be available to the student on a call-up basis, but the student will never be required to trudge through such an explanation because the computer felt it was needed.

3. Communicative CALL will allow and encourage the student to generate original utterances rather than merely manipulate prefabricated language. Argues Rosenbaum, who worked on the Stony Brook project, "A language learning task should require the student to take a creative action in the target language—i.e., either to generate an utterance or to produce a response based on comprehension of an utterance" (Rosenbaum 1969, 458).

4. Communicative CALL will not try to judge and evaluate everything the student does. Says Terrell, "If we are to raise our expectations for . . . competence in communication, we must lower our expectations for structural accuracy" (1977, 325).

5. Communicative CALL will avoid telling students they are "wrong." Very often when a program tells a student "wrong, try again," the student's answer is not really wrong, it has simply not been anticipated by the programmer. If errors are to be processed at all, the program should endeavor to help the student, either by modeling a well-formed response or by giving gentle hints in that direction.

6. Communicative CALL will not try to "reward" students with congratulatory messages, lights, bells, whistles, or other such nonsense. When the student is using language to try to solve a problem or achieve some goal, success will be sufficient reward in itself.

7. Communicative CALL will not try to be "cute." "One is struck," says Decker, "by the 'talkiness' that has characterized a good deal of programming for CAI, especially in the Humanities fields; quite to the contrary, our hunch has been that students will want to use computer programs in proportion to their conciseness" (1976, 263). Terry's French program, MONIQUE, unwittingly provides examples of what we want to avoid; computer responses to correct answers in his French program include "Oh, la la. Eet eez right" and "Outta sight." (Terry 1977; one might ask, among other things, why these responses are not in French.) And inserting the student's name throughout the program usually ends up sounding phony or patronizing ("Good, Johnny, now try the next one").

8. Communicative CALL will use the target language exclusively. PRACTICANDO ESPANOL CON LA MANZANA II uses about ten times as much English as Spanish. Higgins and Johns (1984, 51) describe a French program in which, in a three- or four-minute sample, the computer uses 174 English words and ten French words; the student, meanwhile, produces sixteen words of English and five of French. Like a good language teacher, the CALL programmer should find ways to communicate with the user without reverting either to English or "computerese." Besides, there is an obvious marketing advantage to a piece of software that does not depend on the user having a particular native language background.

9. Communicative CALL will be flexible. The original teaching machines consisted of a kind of programmed text that would roll past the student as long as she kept punching the right answers; there was, in every case, only one right answer. Many CALL programs seem to be based on the same principle: every stimulus has one and only one response. Computers do not have to be any more "rigid and inhuman" than the people who program them.

10. Communicative CALL will allow the student to explore the subject matter. Seymour Papert created a controversy when he argued in *Mindstorms* that the child should program the computer, rather than vice versa (Papert 1980, 5). What he was objecting to, of course, was precisely the "wrong-try-again" type of computer-assisted instruction we have been describing, the type that usually led the child by the nose through the lesson. Instead, he argues, children should guide themselves through the material. In fact, with LOGO, the language he created for children to explore "turtle geometry," there is no predetermined material of any sort, but rather an environment in which discoveries can be made, discoveries about angles, distance, shapes, etc.

Exploratory CALL can offer the student an environment in which to play with language or manipulate it to see how things go together. I think many of us have discovered as language teachers (perhaps as students) that learning a language requires a strong sense of play, and that we are never in fact far from the ridiculous. Perhaps it is the nature of the species that we seem to delight in playing with words: pig latin, tongue twisters, puns, even poetry is often primarily linguistic play. Of course in exploratory programs of this sort there would be no predetermined "right" answers—perhaps no answers at all.

11. Communicative CALL will create an environment in which using the target language feels natural, both on screen and off. An important source of comprehensible input that is often overlooked in the discussion of computer materials is the communication that usually takes place, not between computer and user, but between users. Programs tend to be used by small groups, often pairs, of students, rather than by students working alone. Invariably the students get involved in much healthy discussion centering on how you make the thing work or the best way to solve the problem. This discussion tends to be increasingly in the target language to the extent that (1) the program itself says everything in the target language, (2) the students understand the mechanics of running the program and can concentrate on the content. With each running, this off-screen discussion will require less of the native language. Some programs will, by their design, lend themselves especially well to this sort of group activity, notably the more open-ended simulations and problem-solving activities.

12. Communicative CALL will never try to do anything that a book could do just as well. (This rule should apply to any use of the computer.) We do not need to create electronic page-turners which simply fill the screen with text. Nor do we need electronic workbooks whose only "advantage" is that they tell the students when their answers are "wrong."

13. Above all, communicative CALL will be fun. One thing that killed the language lab was making it a requirement. If our CALL programs are not attractive enough that students will want to run them, maybe we should shelve them and start over. CALL work should be optional, supplementary work. No exams or quizzes should be given on the computer. And there is no need for checking up to see what students do on the computer beyond finding out if the programs are running as they should. Of course the computer is capable of a lot of record-keeping: who has logged on for how long, how many wrong answers they gave, etc. But this kind of supervision seems to be more intimidating than helpful, especially since one of the principal advantages of the computer over the personal tutor is that students know they need not feel embarrassed or anxious if they have to do the same exercise five times before they get it right. We need to let students explore, experiment, learn (and enjoy doing it), without the obsessive concern for constant evaluation that seems to bog down so much of what goes on in education. For Leonard, computers will (someday) free education for much more creative things; in the meantime,

> All these projects [PLATO, Stanford, etc.], in comparison to what they can become, must be looked upon as crude and rudimentary. They lack, most of all, a sense of fun, of play, of sheer delight. Their developers may be too enthralled with the hardware itself to view that rare if urgent vision of learning as ecstatic, as an art form (Leonard 1968, p. 189f.).

6.2 COMMUNICATIVE CALL: EXAMPLES

As soon as we free ourselves from the "wrong-try-again" model, we find that there are indeed innovative, interesting, and challenging ways to use a computer. In this section, we consider a number of programs (or ideas for programs) that meet at least some of our criteria for communicative CALL.

6.2.1 Simulations

Simulations allow the user to act out a real-life experience on the computer, whether it is managing a nuclear power plant or dissecting a frog; the most elaborate simulations are the systems used to teach pilots to fly airliners. From a language point of view, using a simulation is using linguistic competence as a means to an end, such as solving a problem, rather than as an end in itself. The problem might be something as practical as getting from A to B on a map of Madrid or planning a trip to France. The student of course needs to use grammar to solve it, but her attention is focused on meaning.

Higgins (1983b, 5) describes a simulation program called PHOTOFIT. The computer draws a face by using random combinations of certain prestored facial features (eyes, moustaches, etc.). The user, like a witness to a crime, must learn the face and then "tell" the computer how to redraw it. As the user gives commands ("nose, bigger"), the drawing reappears on the screen. Later the results are compared with the original drawing, and the computer "debriefs" the user on the points of difference. The point is quite simply to use language to achieve a goal.

In a simulation, of course, the program will not call attention to errors or attempt to "correct" them. The principle in operation here is the one we pointed out in Chapter 2, namely that correction should not intrude in a communicative activity. Failure to input the proper linguistic forms results quite simply in failure to communicate ("I do not understand; write it another way"), as in real life. Needless to say, this approach also considerably simplifies the programming task.

6.2.2 Communicative Games

The only real difference between a game program and a non-game program appears to be that the user perceives it is a game. Beyond that, there must be an obstacle to overcome and a goal to be reached. Hence a game is a type of simulation. Games are not only motivating, they encourage social interaction and, as we have pointed out, a good bit of genuinely communicative language use ("Why don't you try typing it in this way?").

Some games are obviously much more useful than others. The ever-present HANGMAN is not a good example of a communicative game, since it clearly entails little more than random guessing of letters and involves very little real manipulation of language. In addition, as has been pointed out, in HANGMAN "it is more interesting to make a mistake than to answer correctly" (Hope et al. 1984, 40). At least one computer version of the game does not even give the student any "man" to "hang" (see review in Culley and Mulford 1983, 24).

A better example is MYSTERY HOUSE (Sierra On-Line Systems, 1982), a French translation of an English adventure game with relatively sophisticated graphics. The student enters the house, seen on the screen, and works her way through it, picking up clues and trying to solve the various crimes that have taken place. She communicates with the computer by giving two-word commands such as "Ouvrez porte" and so on. (It is perhaps unfortunate that the program does not employ sufficient parsing strategies to enable it to understand—indeed, insist on—the more grammatical "ouvrez la porte.") What makes the program attractive is that it is highly interactive, gets the user involved in what is going on, and—crucially—is focused on meaning rather than form. The student uses language to communicate instructions, rather than simply to fill in a blank. (MYSTERY HOUSE is not without its bugs, however. In a Fall 1983 computer workshop, I watched two French teachers get hopelessly stuck at one point in the program, simply because they could not figure out the wording the program wanted for the instruction they wanted to give—a good example of inflexible programming.)

The popular exploratory game, ADVENTURE, lends itself very nicely to language practice when translated. As in MYSTERY HOUSE, the player moves through a maze by giving commands such as "Go south," "Take the key," "Climb the stairs," etc. As Higgins points out, "Part of the fun is finding out what instructions the computer understands . . . as well as exploring the maze, you explore the language" (Higgins 1983b, 6). One French version of such a game, known as LA GRANDE AVENTURE, offers a good example of a sound communicative activity with pedagogical flaws. The program is highly interactive: the student proceeds step by step by giving commands, asking for more information, even sidetracking to try different alternatives. Yet reviewers felt that the program was far too tolerant regarding the form of the French input. It accepts only two-word input, and it reads only the first five letters of each word typed in, meaning that it accepts things like "sorte maiso" for "sortez de la maison." In addition, according to reviewers, it introduces too much unfamiliar, low-frequency vocabulary. Nevertheless, it was felt that programs of this sort had "great potential" for acquisition practice (Culley and Mulford 1983, 29–31). As Higgins and Johns point out (1984, 66), ADVENTURE provides "a context in which 'reading for meaning' [has] a very clear and definite purpose."

6.2.3 Text Manipulation Programs

Clearly one way to make a language program more meaningful is to use texts that go beyond the simple sentence level, providing context and a form of comprehensible input. Yet if the program does nothing more than turn pages, there is no real advantage over a book. What a computer can do well, and fast, is manipulate the text in a variety of ways. Nelson (1970) suggested what he called "hypertext" (branching or performing text), one version of which is "stretchtext." At the user's command, the writing on the screen changes; the text opens up and words and phrases, relative clauses, etc., are popped in and out of the gaps. The student can stretch the text out, then compress it back to its original form:

```
Stretchtext is a form of writing.  It is read from
a screen.

Stretchtext, a kind of hypertext, is  basically  a
form  of  writing  closely  related  to other prose.
It is read by a user or student  from  a  computer
display screen.
```

Nelson's point is that the computer allows for a new kind of dynamic interaction between reader and text. Words are no longer stuck to the page; students can be encouraged to play with them, move them about, explore possibilities. For example, a narrative passage in French could be made more personal, hence more meaningful, if students could manipulate the characters and events to suit their fancy, along the lines of the suggestions that are often made for "controlled composition." Manipulation could begin at the level of simple substitution: the user changes the principal character from Jean to Jeanne and then makes all the corresponding gender changes that are necessary in the story. A longer program might imitate the "write-your-own" adventure books that are now popular with young readers. In these stories, the reader is given options at various exciting moments in the story: "If you decide to explore the cave, turn to page 23. If you decide to go back to camp, turn to page 25." Such "branching" stories would lend themselves very well to a dynamic computer reading exercise, with the reader always in control of the reading.

Weibel (1980) describes a reading program that provides a unique form of comprehensible input. His German program starts out with largely English paragraphs written with German syntax plus a few German words that can be understood from the context. As the program progresses, it gradually increases the ratio of German to English. Although some might object to the mix of languages (and the somewhat contorted syntax), the texts are highly comprehensible when read in sequence. The program would be even more meaningful if the student could pop the German words in and out, in the manner of "hypertext."

One variation on text manipulation comprises programs that contain a prewritten text which the student does not see at first but must reconstruct. Higgins' STORYBOARD (Higgins 1983b) is such a program. The computer simply presents a screenful of dashes and a title. The student must guess what words are in the passage, hangman style, but with words instead of letters. With each correct guess the word is printed in everywhere it occurs in the text. As the game goes on, guessing words depends more and more on global understanding of both meaning and form.

Cloze programs, such as CLOZEMASTER, work much the same way. The teacher types text into the computer. The computer automatically deletes every fifth or sixth word and leaves a blank in its place. The computer remembers the words that have been deleted, and it is the student's task to figure them out. It could also be programmed to accept reasonable synonyms in place of the original word. Again, the cloze exercise involves using language in a larger context and is thus, at least in part, a communicative activity. (A nice variation on this exercise would be to have the student listen to the same passage on a computer-controlled tape player (see Section 6.4.1) and then fill in the missing words.)

6.2.4 Text Generation Programs

In a text generation program the student creates an original text with the computer's help. In this case there will be no prefabricated text in the system, and the computer will be incapable of passing judgment on the final product. The usefulness of the exercise depends on the quality of the help the student receives.

Several programs can generate simple poems (or poem-like text, for those who prefer to think that poetry is a strictly human undertaking) by asking the student to provide words of various parts of speech. COMPU-POEM (Marcus 1981) formats the student's words and phrases into a haiku-like structure:

```
The tree house
        full of childhoodmemories
    suspended on the lonely oak tree
        softly, in a whisper
swaying.
```

Although the program was intended to help native English speakers learn to express themselves, it clearly would also help ESL students understand the different parts of speech and what they do. Papert cites the example of a young girl who, after working with a program much like COMPUPOEM, suddenly announced, "Now I know why we have nouns and verbs!" (Papert 1980, 48).

MADLIB (Ahl 1975), much like the popular party game, uses a partially prefabricated story frame with missing nouns or adjectives. The student is prompted for words of a specified part of speech and then is shown the completed story that results. The effect can be fun: "Come up to my (piano) and see my (banana), she said." And the student learns, unwittingly perhaps, to identify the parts of speech, and finds out what happens when you use the wrong one ("Come up to my (grouchy) and see my (shiny), she said").

6.2.5 Other "Communicative" Formats

A CALL program can be made more meaningful in many other ways. For example, several program authors have experimented with using more context in language exercises. Holmes (1980) describes an alternative to the common vocabulary translation (or flashcard) drill. First students must study the vocabulary in the book and read the passage in which the words or phrases are used. On the computer, students then see short (one- or two-sentence) passages with blanks where the vocabulary items from the lesson should go. If they type in a wrong answer, the definition of the item (in the target language) is automatically displayed, and students can try again. Students can also ask to see the definition the first time if they have no idea. One note of flexibility built into the program: if the answer is valid, but not one from the lesson, the computer acknowledges it as correct and asks the student to think of another example.

Another useful format would involve the simple variant of practicing structure while asking questions about content (cf. Hope et al. 1984). For example, the Spanish verb *ir* might be practiced with questions such as:

```
COMPUTER:   ?Ado'nde van Uds. los domingos (parque,
            iglesia, playa, escuela)?

Student:    Vamos a la iglesia.
```

Alternatively, the computer could present sentences that do not make sense, and ask the student to "correct" them:

```
            Voy a la escuela los domingos.
```

```
Voy a la escuela en avio'n.

Vamos a la iglesia los martes.
```

Or the computer could present a short passage, a mini-paragraph, accompanied by questions—on content, not form. If it used computer graphics (see Section 6.4.2), the program could present a story with pictures and ask questions about it. Ideally the program would allow for a fairly wide range of possible answers on the content, and would not get picky on grammar beyond "No entiendo" when it simply could not make any sense out of it.

A few other examples of programs I would like to see include:

— Dialog with words or phrases missing: Students complete the conversation in a way that makes sense. The computer would allow for a range of possible responses that fit the context.

— Cued dialog: Given a certain communicative situation, the student constructs a possible dialog, following the computer's cues (cf. Allen and Valette 1977, 311):

```
Au restaurant

Garcon:  De'sirez?

Client:  Spe'cialite'?

Garcon:  Biftek.

Client:  Alors.

Garcon:  Vin?

Client:  Rouge.
```

Following each cue, the student writes in the appropriate line of dialog. When finished, the computer displays the student's dialog in one piece and then displays its own (prestored) version for comparison. Rather than having the program attempt to "understand" or "correct" the student's dialog, the student would be invited to go back and edit her own. The advantage of doing it this way is that "a more powerful intelligence than the computer is used to compare the right answer with the student answer" (Hope et al. 1984).

— A multi-media listening-reading-writing exercise: (1) Using audio and some form of visuals, perhaps computer graphics, the computer narrates a story. (2) The student is asked a series of "and then what happened?" questions which enable her to retell the story. (3) The program parses the student's answers in an attempt to understand her version, and prompts her to rewrite or explain her answers wherever it fails. (4) Based on the program's understanding of this retelling, it redisplays the original animated drawings in the now-revised sequence and comments on any substantial differences between the two versions. For the student, the object is not to try to "get it right" or score 25 out of 30, but simply to practice putting words together in a meaningful way.[2]

6.3 COMMUNICATIVE CALL: THE COMMON DENOMINATOR

Most of the programs or program ideas just described have several characteristics in common which are worth noting here. They show little or no concern for structuring or sequencing material in terms of the customary grammatical syllabus. If they attempt to judge or evaluate what the student does, it is more to provide helpful hints than to suggest "you're wrong, I'm right." The student is, for the most part, in control of the flow of events and is allowed to relate directly to the subject matter in a personal way. Rather than binding the student to a predetermined or prefabricated lesson, the program tries to free the student to create her own learning experience. The computer serves as facilitator, not taskmaster, and the student senses that the program, because of its game-like nature, is not simply one more required exercise, but rather an interesting and motivating supplement, an extra. Finally, the program does not try to duplicate or simulate what goes on in the classroom, but it creates instead a novel activity that would be difficult if not impossible to do without a computer.[3]

6.4 WHERE DO WE GO FROM HERE?

Even such "communicative" programs by no means exhaust the technological resources that are available. In fact, we are just beginning to imagine the pedagogical possibilities of most of the computer-related devices that surround us. Yet one is reluctant to overemphasize hardware. Like the language lab before it, educational software has yet to live up to the technological promise of the machines themselves. We should be careful not to be so impressed by the latest electronic gadget that we forget what it is we are trying to do. We need to think, as Barrutia says, "not in terms of grander hardware, but rather in terms of making the hardware conform to grander and more humanistic programs" (Barrutia 1970, 361). One of the promising directions for more humanistic programs will be systems that make use of artificial intelligence strategies so that the computer can, in a more complete sense, "understand" the student's input and produce a more individualized and more communicative interaction. Chapter 7 examines some of the possibilities for creating such programs.

We can nevertheless reasonably inquire what else the hardware can do for us. The two most obvious areas that we have not explored in much detail thus far involve the use of sound and pictures.

6.4.1 Sound

Today's language teaching methodology, as we noted in Chapter 3, stresses the importance of listening comprehension. For most methods, it is the first skill used; for many, it is the only skill employed in the early stages. For this reason, we argued that the most promising use of the language lab was as a source of comprehensible input for listening. For the same reason, developers of language software need to explore better ways of incorporating some sort of audio response.

There are basically three ways in which sound can accompany a computer. The simplest is the computer-controlled cassette player, much-used in the PLATO IV system and an integral part of software packages such as the Atari materials. A signal from the program causes the recorder to play a designated segment of tape. In PLATO, audio tapes can be random-accessed, which means that any passage on the tape can be located and played at any time, though of course any audio response produced this way is necessarily prerecorded. An alternative is to store prerecorded messages in digital form on the floppy disk itself along with the rest of the program. A device available for the Apple II known as Supertalker allows audio messages to be stored in this fashion. This is less complicated mechanically than the cassette system, and access is much faster. One problem with digitized audio, however, is that it takes up a lot of memory space. One program using the Supertalker has room for only a total of twenty-four seconds of prerecorded audio (Culley and Mulford 1983, 27).

Eventually the most interesting approach to audio may well be through speech synthesis. All sorts of devices are learning to "talk." Texas Instruments made a breakthrough of sorts with its "Speak and Spell" toy, which can spell out words audibly and then announce if they are correctly spelled. IBM markets a typewriter for the blind that pronounces a sentence or word once it has been typed in (if the word is not in its lexicon, it spells it). In a CALL system, once the program determined the appropriate response to be transmitted to the student, a separate speech synthesizer, using phonological rules, would translate this response into a digitized phonetic code much like the one used to store canned audio; this code could then be output as sound. Output would closely resemble speech in most respects, although intonation contours would probably be somewhat flat. But the object of audio feedback would not be so much to provide a letter-perfect pronunciation model as to offer the student's "dumb tutor" a chance to say something once in a while, and to provide much-needed listening comprehension practice and more comprehensible input. At this stage, however, it is difficult to speculate how practical such a system would be.

Technically even more difficult is speech recognition by computer. Speech recognition systems must be "trained" to understand a particular voice and normally cannot handle more than one or two words at a time. As the technology advances, however, it may well prove to be a promising addition to CALL. At least one researcher is experimenting with computer analysis of ESL students' intonation contours; the program displays the intonation contour of the student's utterance on the screen along with the teacher's model for comparison (Loritz 1984).

6.4.2 Pictures

The addition of visual images to a CALL program would obviously do much to make that program both more meaningful and more interesting to use. A number of different approaches have been tried, none of which has proven entirely successful. PLATO IV originally had equipment that could retro-project random-access microfiche images on top of computer displays. Because of a number of technical problems, the system was never widely used. Others have experimented with computer-controlled slide projectors; although they lack the random-access capability and thus can only move in forward-backward sequence, they allow the computer to project the appropriate image as needed. As a medium, though, slides tend to be somewhat clumsy to handle.

6.4.2.1 Computer Graphics

The most promising work dealing with visual images has employed either computer graphics or computer-controlled video. Computer graphics means embedding a set of commands in the program to make the computer generate preset images at the appropriate moment. Although these images are usually fairly primitive line drawings, they have several advantages. Unlike fiches, slides, or video, computer graphics require no extra equipment. Images can appear together with text on the screen, and can be moved about, recalled to the screen as needed, and altered at will for size, color, and so on. Access to the images is entirely random.

But computer graphics also have distinct disadvantages, which may explain why their use is not as widespread as one would have imagined. They are, as we have noted, primitive, often not nearly as "high resolution" as their developers claim. It is certainly questionable whether an unclear, ambiguous image is better than no image at all. The more detail that is programmed into the image, the more expensive and time-consuming it becomes—time-consuming both in the amount of time it takes for the programmer to produce it, and the amount of time it takes for the computer to generate it.

Courseware using relatively sophisticated graphics, such as LE REPAS in French (D. C. Heath 1983), also tends to have little room left on the disk for much language practice and is usually considerably more expensive than other programs which may well offer a much greater variety of activities. The BIPACS software package reviewed in the Culley and Mulford volume (1983, 25–27), although it uses graphics "in a more imaginative and thoroughgoing way than in any other courseware we reviewed," was found to be extremely limited in the quantity of linguistic material, offering "only the spottiest coverage of any imaginable curriculum," and is inordinately expensive for what it does. Atari's much-advertised CONVERSATIONAL FRENCH (and Spanish and German) is a good example of using color graphics in a pedagogically trivial program. Apart from providing pictures to go with a set of disembodied sentences and checking to see if the user can associate the appropriate picture with its sentence, the programs do little that would not be better done with cassette tapes and a good book. Concluded one reviewer, "The designers of the program apparently thought that if you take a grammar-oriented text and put on a sound and light show with it, you will automatically have a conversational program" (Culley and Mulford 1983, 21).

6.4.2.2 Video

Because it incorporates both visual images and sound, computer-controlled video offers a promising, if expensive, alternative to computer graphics. The combination of television-quality pictures and a full sound track provides maximum comprehensibility of input, plus the opportunity to incorporate authentic cultural content, to re-create, in fact, the cultural environment in which the language is spoken. The advantage of videodisc, as opposed to videotape, is the random access feature. Videotape, like audio cassette tape, is linear; it can only start, stop, go forward, or go backward. Finding any particular image, particularly if it happens to be on the other end of the tape, can be time-consuming. Extensive branching between various parts of the tape would be clumsy at best. Videodisc allows the accessing of any one of the disc's 54,000 individual frames (still images) within 3 seconds. These images can be displayed either as stills or as motion picture segments, accompanied by audio tracks. The potential is vividly evident in the latest arcade games, which employ a combination of computer-controlled videodisc and computer graphics. One such "laserdisc" game, known as "M.A.C.H. 3," superimposes player-controlled graphics on live-action film footage shot from a jet plane; the overall effect makes Pac-Man look like Parcheesi.[4]

The most elaborate CALL experiment with videodisc to date is the "Montevidisco" project at Brigham Young University (Gale 1983). The student user "visits" a town in northern Mexico and "talks" to the natives who appear on the screen. When the natives ask questions in Spanish, the image freezes to give the student time to respond. Options for responses appear on the screen. The student chooses the desired response, speaks into the microphone (the oral response is recorded for later evaluation by the instructor), and the program continues, branching according to the student's response. In this sense it is like an adventure game—the sequence of events, where the student goes, etc., depends on the student's choices. (Note that the computer does not in any way process or "understand" the student's oral input, only the corresponding typed choice.) As students explore the village in full color and sound, the Spanish they are exposed to is perhaps the ultimate in comprehensible input.

A variation on this idea, and one that would be considerably less complicated to implement, has been suggested by Earl Stevick (personal communication). One could take a scene from the videodisc version of an existing target-language movie and program it to play in sentence-length segments, each meaningful in itself, but in no particular order. Students working in groups would take notes, replay the segments, and consult with each other to try to figure out the order in which the segments should run. Any particular sequence could be called up and viewed again by typing in key words that it contained. Once two consecutive segments had been correctly placed relative to each other, the computer would thereafter treat them as a unit for purposes of recall. Not only would the students be manipulating a good deal of authentic language, they would obviously have to use a lot of their own in the process.

For the teacher with video but no computer, an even simpler suggestion: rent or buy a videotape copy of a good target-language movie with motivating narrative and plenty of dialog, and treat it as you would any good literary text. An ESL teacher I know shows "West Side Story" to his students. After crucial scenes, he stops the tape and asks questions such as "What did he do?" "What would you have done?" "What do you think will happen next?" etc. Motivation couldn't be higher.

6.5 ALTERNATIVES TO CALL

6.5.1 Text Editing

The foreign language teacher interested in exploring the use of computers should not assume that CALL—even of the communicative kind—is the whole story. To date the best language-related use of these multi-purpose machines is still word processing. The best "program" for helping students to write in a foreign language (or in their own) may well be a text editing program such as Wordstar, Selectwriter, etc. Experiments with using word processing in composition classes have shown that the ease with which students can produce and edit neat, uniform text tends to encourage them to write more and to edit more of what they write. Students could learn to write in a foreign language on the computer by first copying a prepared text and then transforming the text according to a model. As the writing becomes more and more their own, the teacher will want to avoid inhibiting student expression by overcorrecting their work (the red pencil syndrome), but instead encourage them to correct their own as best they can (a process that usually turns out to be highly motivating on the computer).

6.5.2 Electronic Mail

As more and more colleges have computer terminals or networked microcomputers at various locations around campus, we could begin to explore the possibilities of using electronic mail for language practice. Electronic mail is a means of sending messages from one computer terminal to another, usually over telephone lines. The receiver does not have to be present to read incoming messages, since the system will save them until needed. Students could send foreign language messages to each other or to their instructor as a writing exercise. Foreign language faculty at Mills College will begin experimenting during 1984–85 with such a system for homework practice. Modeled after the successful work that has been done with "dialog journals" (Staton 1983), the project will have students send short, personal, conversational messages to their instructor on a daily basis. If in English, an entry might look like this:

> I am worry about the test. I no understan the part what you explain us today in the class. Can you explain me this?

Instead of correcting or editing these messages, the instructor will simply reply with comments; the form of the reply, however, will attempt to include examples of the structures that the student may have had trouble with, much like the "modeling" we discussed earlier as a substitute for classroom correction of mistakes:

> I know you are worried about the test. There are other students who don't understand the part that I explained in class today. I will try to find a better way to explain it to you tomorrow. OK?

Students will keep a running file of their messages and will be expected to go back and edit them as best they can after reading the responses. It is hoped that the ability to produce clean copy, the quick response to their messages, and the ease with which they can correct them will encourage students to write more and to be more critical of their own writing. And, of course, to the extent that the students are encouraged to write original and personal messages, the writing exercise can be a very meaningful and communicative one.

6.6 SUMMARY: ALTERNATIVES TO "WRONG-TRY-AGAIN"

It is much too early to assume that we have seen everything there is to see in computer-assisted language learning. We need to challenge the skeptics and pessimists who would have us believe that the programmed-instruction model is the only way it can be done. Clearly we can do much better—better than "wrong, try again," better than HANGMAN, better than slickly packaged commercial programs that are more dazzle than substance. We must find, or create, programs that allow our students to explore the richness and depth of language rather than merely manipulate relatively superficial grammatical detail. We need to see the computer less as a teacher directing and judging the student's behavior, and more as a helper or facilitator creating an environment in which the student can explore the language, play with it, or simply try it out. Just as Papert's LOGO creates an environment in which children quite naturally use geometry to solve problems (for the most part without realizing it's geometry), a good CALL program will set up an environment in which language—real language—is needed, both on the screen and in front of it. Some of the programs in this chapter show how this might be done, how programs can be made both more "communicative" and more sensible. Chapter 7, on artificial intelligence, carries the notion of "communication" one step further.

NOTES TO CHAPTER 6

1. Note that I am using the term "communicative" here somewhat loosely. Strictly speaking, mere contextualization of language is not in itself communication. Communication is the exchange of information. As Stevick points out, describing what is obvious in a picture adds no new information to the picture, hence nothing is communicated (1982, 130). Such an activity would be an example of what Paulston (1980) calls "meaningful drill": the learner must understand what she is saying, but the content of the response is already known. In contrast, in a "communicative drill" the learner adds new information about the real world, even though the structures she uses may be controlled. Although most of the CALL activities described in this chapter would fall into the "communicative" category, there are also some useful exercises of the "meaningful" type.

2. I am indebted to an anonymous reviewer for suggesting improvements in this example.

3. For further examples of communicative programs, including several different types of simulations, see Higgins and Johns (1984).

4. Note, however, that for all the technological advantages of videodisc, it has failed to compete commercially with the video cassette recorder. RCA has already announced plans to withdraw its videodisc player from the market.

chapter

7

Artificial Intelligence and CALL

7.1 COMPUTERS AND NATURAL LANGUAGE

In the 1983 movie "Wargames," the computer whiz hero, David, has a system that talks to him by means of a speech synthesizer. "How does it know what to say?" his girlfriend asks. "It says whatever it is programmed to say," replies David. Not entirely accurate, but the point is well taken: computers are dumb machines with no inherent, built-in way to understand natural (i.e., human) language. They do not "know" anything beyond strings of ones and zeros and whether these strings are the same as or different from other strings. Computer "understanding" comes only as the result of clever and relatively complicated programming.

Natural language, as we saw in Chapter 1, is highly complex. Beyond the morphological and syntactic complexity inherent in the rules that we all somehow manage to internalize lies the murky world of meaning—many-layered, subtle, and often ambiguous. Computer handling of human language, or "natural language processing," is still primitive by comparison. There are to date no systems which can fully parse (i.e., analyze the structure of) freely created sentences, let alone understand what they mean.

Nevertheless, work on natural language processing, a branch of artificial intelligence (AI), has experienced limited success in some areas. Programs have been written which can compare the language of *Hamlet* with that of *Macbeth*, or analyze news stories to detect trends or patterns. Of particular interest to us is the work in simulated dialog, programs that parse input and generate some sort of meaningful response. Winograd developed a system known as SHRDLU which could understand extremely intricate English sentences having to do with its mini-universe of colored blocks (Winograd 1972). Programs have been written that can "talk" about baseball ("Who won the world series in 1927?") or the weather ("What is the high today in Des Moines?"). In a more serious vein, linguists are currently working on what they call "English front ends"—language understanding programs that will allow computer users to communicate directly with the computer in normal English sentences rather than computer talk.

One of the best-known conversational programs is called ELIZA (Weizenbaum 1976), after the woman in Shaw's *Pygmalion* who was taught to talk "right." Developed in 1966 by computer scientist Joseph Weizenbaum of MIT, ELIZA could carry on a plausible conversation with a human typing at a terminal. The topic of conversation would depend on the nature of ELIZA's "script," the most famous of which was DOCTOR, designed to simulate ("parody" is the term Weizenbaum uses) the role of a non-directive therapist in a consultation by responding to the user's "complaints" (ELIZA's responses are given in uppercase):

(1)   I'm very unhappy these days.

   I AM SORRY TO HEAR YOU ARE UNHAPPY

   The problem is my father

   TELL ME MORE ABOUT YOUR FATHER

   My father thinks I am lazy

   DOES ANYONE ELSE IN YOUR FAMILY THINK YOU ARE LAZY

   Everyone picks on me

   ARE YOU THINKING OF SOMEONE IN PARTICULAR

What is taking place here is not "understanding" but simply the appearance of understanding deriving from the clever use of key words and a technique known as "pattern matching." For example, "I am X" is a pattern which allows the computer to respond with a prefabricated pattern of its own, "You say you are X." If X contains a word labeled in the program as negative, such as *unhappy* or *depressed,* the response could then be "I am sorry to hear you are X." When ELIZA gets something she cannot handle, she hedges ("Why do you say that?" or "Go on") or changes the subject by introducing some standard topic ("You haven't mentioned your mother"). We will return to ELIZA's strategies in Section 7.3.

7.2 ARTIFICIAL INTELLIGENCE IN CALL PROGRAMS

As we have seen, most CALL programs have not gone very far in the direction of artificial intelligence, nor have they experimented with anything resembling ELIZA's "conversation." Although the original report on the Stony Brook project (Adams et al. 1968) was entitled "Conversation with a Computer as a Technique of Language Instruction," it turns out that "conversation" means only typing in verb forms.

A handful of programs have experimented with AI strategies of one sort or another. Sanders (1983) describes an "intelligent" game for practicing German. Called SPION, the program is a sort of simulation in which the task is to find the correct route from the West Berlin airport to town. This is done by asking the program questions or giving instructions to try options. Along the way, the student must find and interpret clues needed to gain access to secret information. The program not only has the capacity to understand student input, it can also recognize grammar mistakes of certain kinds.

Another German program uses AI strategies to help students with the writing of complete sentences (Weischedel et al. 1978). The sentences are written in response to questions on a dialog. The program uses a set of internal rules plus a lexicon of some 200 words to detect misused vocabulary, syntax problems, misspellings, plus well-formed answers with factual errors. Unfortunately, however, the computer still plays the role of the teacher who knows all the answers rather than that of facilitator or helper.

Sometimes very complicated systems are used to perform simple, even trivial, tasks. Cerri and Breuker (1981) describe a system called DART which can be used to develop intelligent CALL programs. DART is apparently capable of analyzing student input for meaning, and thus detecting and diagnosing misconceptions regarding the linguistic data. In their prototype program, called ELISA (not ELIZA, note), these sophisticated strategies are nonetheless used for no better purpose than to provide "smart" error processing in a translation drill focusing on subordinating conjunctions.

One alternative to the computer as taskmaster is the program that allows the student to ask the questions for a change, and requires the computer to come up with the answers. One such program is Higgins' GRAMMARLAND (Higgins 1983b, 6). I recently developed a similar experimental question-answering program inspired by Higgins' model. Called QUESTIONS, the program has built into it a certain amount of information about a room in a house; this is what it "knows." The object is to ask enough questions to obtain a full description of the room, full enough to draw a floorplan with all the furnishings in their proper place. To do this requires asking a lot of questions, definitely a meaningful form of language practice:

(2)   Student: Are there any chairs?

        COMPUTER: Yes.

        Student: How many chairs are there?

        COMPUTER: There are three.

        Student: Where are the chairs?

        COMPUTER: Two of them are under the north window, the other is to the left of the fireplace.

        Student: Is there a table in the room?

        COMPUTER: Yes.

If the student asks about something that is not in the room, the computer "knows" by elimination, and says so. If the question simply cannot be understood, it says "I don't understand." No attempt is made to "correct" the student's input, since grammaticality is quite beside the point. If it is correct enough to be understood, it has served its purpose.

7.3 A SPANISH ELIZA

It would perhaps be useful for the reader to take a closer look at what goes into software of this type, what the problems are, and how they are solved. In doing so, you will note that, although the problems are complex, their solutions are ultimately more linguistic than computational.

The programs I feel most qualified to discuss in such detail are the ones I have worked on. The next two sections of this chapter are devoted to an analysis of a CALL project outlined in an earlier publication (Underwood 1982). In that article I describe an experimental, simulated conversation program which borrows freely from the pattern-matching strategies of ELIZA-type programs. Like the original ELIZA, it is written in LISP (in many ways similar to LOGO, which is itself written in LISP) in two somewhat autonomous parts: (1) a language analyzer, which contains input routines for analyzing the user's sentences, and (2) a script, a kind of lexicon that lists the key words to be looked for, plus sentence frames for use in composing responses.

In designing this Spanish ELIZA, I discovered some interesting technical problems having to do with the nature of the Spanish sentence (beyond the obvious problem of the accent marks and the tildes). To start with, Spanish subject pronouns are clearly of little use as key words, since they are normally not used—it would be highly unnatural for the student to write "yo soy" every time. This means that, in the absence of a subject noun phrase (NP) or reflexive or object pronouns, the verb itself must be the key word. If the contextual framework of the conversation is too wide, one would have to enter an enormous number of verbs as key words, each with a separate routine.

Second, I quickly realized an obvious advantage of English over Spanish, one that follows logically from the fact that English subject pronouns cannot be left out: in a "you-I" conversation, the same verb form will serve for both parties (with the exception of the verb *be*):

(3)   `I need to talk to someone`

                `YOU SAY YOU NEED TO TALK TO SOMEONE`

In the Spanish version, where first-person and second-person forms will always differ, each verb form must have a "translation" declared in ELIZA's lexicon:

(4)   (defprop necesito necesitas translation)

This defprop ("define property") means to the language analyzer that wherever the input sentence contains *necesito,* the response, if it is to use the verb at all, must use *necesitas.*

On the other hand, Spanish has some definite advantages over English. For one, it distinguishes between subject and object in all its personal pronouns; English *you,* crucially, is ambiguous, allowing ELIZA to trip up as in this sequence:

(5)   I don't want to talk to you anymore.

         WHY DON'T YOU WANT TO TALK TO I ANYMORE

Here Eliza has picked up the only translation of *you* that it has, namely *I.* The Spanish version can distinguish between "*tú-yo*" (subject) and "*te-me*" (object):

(6)   No te quiero hablar ma's.

         ?POR QUE' NO ME QUIERES HABLAR MA'S?

What follows is a longer sample of a run with my Spanish version of ELIZA:[1]

(7)   Hola

         HOLA---HA'BLAME UN POCO DE TI

         Me llamo Jennifer

         ?JENNIFER?---ES UN BUEN NOMBRE

         Eres muy simpa'tica

         ?POR QUE' CREES QUE SOY MUY SIMPA'TICA?

         Porque mantienes una conversacio'n interesante

         ?ES ESA LA RAZO'N, DE VERDAD?

         Claro que es

         PARECES MUY SEGURA

         Quiero hablar de mi familia

         MUY BIEN, ADELANTE

         Mi hermana es muy inteligente

         ?QUIE'N MA'S EN TU FAMILIA ES INTELIGENTE?

         Las computadoras me asustan un poco

         ?POR QUE' MENCIONAS LAS COMPUTADORAS?

This is typical ELIZA-the-therapist talk. To be useful as an instructional routine, however, I originally felt that the ELIZA format would need another type of analysis and response: error checking and error messages. Prior to generating a response sentence, the program would need to have some way to check the syntax of the input sentence for a recognizable error and then jump to appropriate error-handling routines. Clearly this would only be possible if the contextual framework of the dialog were very highly restricted, so that the degree of predictability would be high. The problem in machine translation has been precisely the low level of predictability. Current work in natural language computation, as Weizenbaum points out, is more conscious of this problem:

> What sharply distinguishes current work on machine understanding of language from the work of the early 1960's and before is. . . the current strong use of predictions both on the local syntactic level and, more important, on the larger contextual level (Weizenbaum 1976, 191).

7.4 FAMILIA: ELIZA AS TUTOR

Having experimented with a Spanish version of ELIZA with a DOCTOR-type script, I set out to achieve a more exactly defined goal: a conversational program capable of discussing a single topic, and designed to be especially sensitive to a single syntactic problem. Within those narrow limits, it would (I hoped) be somewhat more sophisticated than ELIZA, precisely because its level of predictability would be much higher. The topic I chose was the family; one objective of the program, then, would be to practice all the common kinship terms (*padre* "father," *abuelo* "grandfather," *primo* "cousin," etc.). The syntactic problem to be checked for was the use of the two verbs "to be," SER and ESTAR, for description.

Before the program could be written, the problem with SER and ESTAR had to be explicitly defined. (Although it is somewhat of a digression here, I would like to reflect on the linguistic details to demonstrate the complexity of what might otherwise seem to be a fairly simple task.) I began with a sample of the kinds of things I wanted the student to be able to say, as well as those I wanted to rule out. For some it is a fairly clear case (those marked with asterisks are ungrammatical):

(8)   a. Mi padre es abogado
      b. *Mi padre está abogado

      c. Jane y Eric son primos
      d. *Jane y Eric están primos

      e. Yo soy la menor de la familia
      f. *Yo estoy la menor de la familia

g. Somos de Nueva York
h. *Estamos de Nueva York

i. Mi hermano está en Europa
j. *Mi hermano es en Europa

In (a)–(f) we see that, unlike SER, ESTAR may not take a noun phrase (NP) as complement. And in (g)–(j) it is clear that ESTAR cannot have a prepositional phrase (PP) with *de* as head, whereas SER cannot have a PP with a locative preposition such as *en*.[2]

When the complement is an adjective phrase (AP), however, the situation is often less clear:

(9)   a. Mi hermano es muy joven
       b. Mi padre está muy joven

       c. Mis tíos son simpáticos
       d. Mi hermano está muy simpático estos días

Here the choice of verb depends on considerations that go beyond the sentence: SER, if the adjective describes a quality that is felt to be an inherent characteristic of the subject, ESTAR, if it is not.

To summarize, then, SER can take an NP, an AP considered to be characteristic, and a nonlocative PP. ESTAR, on the other hand, can only take a locative PP (not *de*) and an AP considered to be a nonessential condition. The most difficult part to sort out is of course the area of overlap, namely (9). Here I decided to adopt the strategy of probability, and merely assume that certain adjectives (e.g., *alto, grande, rubio*) are more probably characteristics and thus would be more likely with SER, whereas others (e.g., *triste, contento, cansado*) are more likely to occur with ESTAR. Anything more subtle than that is probably beyond the level of the students for whom the program is intended.

The central programming strategy involves identifying ungrammatical sequences first through top-priority key words. Take the problem of the PPs, for example. To rule out *SER *en* and *ESTAR *de*, *en* and *de* are made first-priority key words. Their presence in an input sentence trips a routine which checks if the preposition is preceded by the wrong verb, in which case an appropriate message is typed out; otherwise, analysis proceeds elsewhere in the sentence. In the original version (Underwood 1982), FAMILIA's messages were of the "I'm-right-you're-wrong" sort. I now prefer gentle hints, much like Terrell's "modeling" or "expansion":

(10)   Mi madre esta' de Boston

        ?QUIERES DECIR QUE TU MADRE ES DE BOSTON?

The tone is suitably nonauthoritarian, and leaves open the possibility that the computer is wrong (which, in fact, is sometimes the case).

For *ESTAR NP the problem consists of detecting the presence of an NP. One way is by tagging determiners (*un, unos, el, los,* etc.), causing a message to be printed out if they occur following ESTAR. But that would not rule out (8b) and (8d) above, where no determiners are present. For things like (8d), the solution is simple: since family terms such as *primos* were already in the lexicon, a rule was written disallowing any such item after ESTAR. For cases such as (8b), the lexicon would need to be expanded to include such things as professions and identify them as NPs. (A program such as this, when actually put into use, would in fact probably have a lexicon which followed rather closely a vocabulary unit in the text, beyond which one would not expect to get many items.)

For the problem of the APs, where the program would have to look beyond the lexical item itself for a definitive decision, I have resorted to tagging two sets of adjectives in the lexicon as [+ser] and [+estar], respectively, to trigger a message such as:

(11)   Estoy muy alto

         ?QUIERES DECIR QUE ERES MUY ALTO?

To handle the essential vocabulary of the lesson, two strategies are used. First, all kinship terms were listed in the lexicon and labeled [+family]. Identifying a family term in the input sentence allows the program to respond by either commenting on the family member mentioned or by introducing still further family terms:

(12) a. Mi hermano es estudiante de medicina

         ?DO'NDE ESTA' TU HERMANO?

     b. Mi madre es de Boston

         ?Y TUS ABUELOS?

(To avoid duplication, I have divided the kinship terms into two sets; one set introduces the other.)

The second strategy is to give the students a chance to ask questions if they do not recognize a family term when it is introduced. Any student response indicating confusion ("No entiendo," "No sé," etc.) will cause a message to be printed out indicating how to get help:

(13) No entiendo

      SI USO UNA PALABRA QUE NO ENTIENDES, ESCRIBE:
      "QUE' ES UN _____?"

```
Que' es un abuelo?

TUS ABUELOS SON LOS PADRES DE TUS PADRES
```

Thus if the students stay at it long enough and ask enough questions, they will eventually practice all the vocabulary in the lesson.

Following is a run (with lines numbered for reference) using the FAMILIA script. (To write a new program requires only changing the script; the language analyzer remains intact.) The student is given repeated opportunities to practice her knowledge of family terms, is helped when she does not know them, and is monitored on the use of SER and ESTAR. Since the program is open-ended, she may practice until she feels confident with all of these items. The student will be instructed at the outset simply to use forms of SER and ESTAR in the present indicative and the vocabulary from the lesson on the family:[3]

(14) 1 Hola

      2 HOLA---VAMOS A HABLAR DE TU FAMILIA

      3 Mi familia esta' en Colorado

      4 ?ENTONCES UDS. SON DE COLORADO?

      5 Bueno, mi madre esta' de Boston

      6 ?QUIERES DECIR QUE TU MADRE ES DE BOSTON?

      7 Mi madre es de Boston

      8 ?Y TUS ABUELOS?

      9 Mis abuelos esta'n en Colorado tambie'n

      10 ?TIENES TI'OS?

      11 No entiendo

      12 SI USO UNA PALABRA QUE NO ENTIENDES, ESCRIBE;
          "QUE' ES UN----?"

      13 ?Que' es un ti'o?

      14 TU TI'O ES EL HERMANO DE UNO DE TUS PADRES

      15 Si', mi ti'a esta' una profesora en Berkeley

      16 ?QUIERES DECIR QUE TU TI'A ES UNA PROFESORA EN
          BERKELEY?

```
```

```
17    Mi ti'a es una profesora
18    ?ALGUIEN MA'S EN TU FAMILIA ES UNA PROFESORA?
```

A few comments on the dialog: Line 16 is an example of correcting one problem but missing another, since the indefinite article is normally deleted with professions: "Es profesora"; again, further marking in the lexicon would be necessary. Note that the program makes the same mistake in line 18, and also repeats the feminine form *profesora*, where one would normally use the unmarked, i.e., masculine, form.

I am not without certain reservations about programs like FAMILIA. For all its sophistication, it still understands very little of what the student types in (pattern-matching is not real parsing), and it makes dumb mistakes. Trying to catch syntax errors can never be entirely successful, either. In light of our discussion in Chapter 6 regarding error checking, I would now be inclined to say that the program might well be just as valuable without any attempt at the hazardous business of error checking.

The interchange in (14) is nonetheless clearly communicative language practice. The student initiates the dialog and controls the direction it will take. The student can start anywhere, restart, ask questions, and seek help. There is no preset pattern to the "conversation"; each dialog will be different, as each person using it is different. And to those who may complain that conversation with a computer is "cold" and "inhuman," I would answer that it is considerably more human or "human-like" than most of the CALL exercises our students are now being subjected to.

7.5 LOOKING AHEAD

When we begin to examine how computers might be used for language practice, we find there is clearly much we can do that goes beyond the trivial manipulation of discrete grammar points and isolated vocabulary items. We are probably just beginning to realize the possibilities. Most experimentation with artificial intelligence strategies has involved the use of large computer systems and would not be adaptable to microcomputers. As micros get more and more powerful, this will no longer be true; for example, there already exist versions of LISP (the AI language) for the Apple II and Atari 800. More and more programmers will experiment with strategies similar to those used in artificial intelligence. Programs will be more complex, will require a more careful analysis of the linguistic facts, will be harder to create—but will be eminently more interesting to use.

We will learn to "talk" to our computers, and we will teach them to "talk" to us. But at the same time we must not overestimate the value of this "conversation." As Bolt (1968, 90) reminds us in an early paper on Socratic

CAI, the most effective learning aid that we have yet discovered is not computer-assisted instruction but "teacher-assisted instruction." There can be no better "communicative" learning environment than the warm and responsive presence of other human beings.

NOTES TO CHAPTER 7

1. Translation of the dialog in (7):
   Hi
   HI--TELL ME A LITTLE ABOUT YOURSELF
   My name is Jennifer
   JENNIFER?--THAT'S A NICE NAME
   You're very nice
   WHY DO YOU THINK I'M VERY NICE?
   Because you keep up an interesting conversation
   IS THAT THE REAL REASON?
   Sure it is
   YOU SEEM VERY CERTAIN
   I want to talk about my family
   OK, GO AHEAD
   My sister is smart
   WHO ELSE IN YOUR FAMILY IS SMART?
   Computers scare me a little
   WHY DO YOU MENTION COMPUTERS?

2. SER *en* NP does occur in certain (less frequent) contexts where the subject is an activity or event, as in *El concierto es en la sala grande* ("The concert is in the large hall"), but never where the subject is a person.

3. Translation of the dialog in (14):
   1 Hi
   2 HI--LET'S TALK ABOUT YOUR FAMILY
   3 My family is in Colorado
   4 SO YOU [pl] ARE FROM COLORADO?
   5 Well, my mother is [estar] from Boston
   6 DO YOU MEAN YOUR MOTHER IS [ser] FROM BOSTON?
   7 My mother is [ser] from Boston
   8 AND YOUR GRANDPARENTS?
   9 My grandparents are in Colorado too
   10 DO YOU HAVE [UNCLES AND AUNTS]?
   11 I don't understand
   12 IF I USE A WORD YOU DON'T UNDERSTAND, WRITE:
      WHAT IS A ___ ___ ?
   13 What is an [uncle]?
   14 YOUR UNCLE IS THE BROTHER OF ONE OF YOUR PARENTS
   15 Yes, my aunt is [estar] a professor in Berkeley
   16 DO YOU MEAN YOUR AUNT IS [ser] A PROFESSOR IN BERKELEY?
   17 My aunt is [ser] a professor
   18 IS ANYONE ELSE IN YOUR FAMILY A PROFESSOR?

chapter

8

Getting Started

8.1 INTRODUCTION

I have argued at some length in favor of using computers in a certain way, what I have called the "communicative" approach, and I have cited examples of programs that in one way or another reflect this approach. Much has been left unsaid, however, about how all this is done—the nuts and bolts of what computer people call "implementation." There are of course two parts to implementation: hardware (the computer itself and all the accessories or peripherals that go with it), and software (programs, instructions to the computer, usually written on thin magnetic disks known as floppy disks or diskettes). Since any recommendation one could make about hardware could become obsolete almost overnight, I will limit myself to a simple rule: Do not buy a computer (or have your school buy a computer) and then figure out what you are going to do with it. Do it the other way around: find something you would really like to do with a computer, something that can only be done (well) with a computer, and then find the machine that does it best.

That leaves software. At first glance, there would appear to be two clearcut ways to go about it: you either write your own or you use someone else's. In fact, it is not that simple. When you buy a book, the distinction between author and user is obvious; with computer software, this distinction gets blurred. Some software can only be run the way it comes. Other programs won't do a thing until the teacher/user puts a good deal of data into them. So buying versus writing (or "authoring") is not actually an either/or question; the question is more "How much do you want to get involved in the writing?"

There are four levels of answers to this question (in descending order of involvement): (1) using a general-purpose programming language, such as BASIC, and designing one's own program pretty much from the ground up; (2) buying and using a CAI "authoring" language, such as PILOT or EnBASIC, which already has certain answer-processing capabilities built in; (3) buying a foreign language authoring system, like DASHER, which only needs to have the foreign language material inserted; or (4) purchasing a ready-made off-the-shelf package that comes complete with language content, answer-processing routines, etc.—sometimes called turnkey programs (you just turn the key and they go). The first two of these require a certain amount of programming know-how, the last two only the ability to type on a computer. Yet, as we shall see, the differences in time and effort are not the only concerns.

8.2 GENERAL-PURPOSE PROGRAMMING LANGUAGES

The main advantage of using a general-purpose programming language is that it gives the user complete control over what the program does. This is also the main disadvantage: the programmer must tell it how to do everything. Not only does this take longer to do, it takes much longer to learn *how* to do. As Otto and Pusack (1983, 26) point out, a good teacher/ programmer might be able to produce a useful vocabulary dictation program in one weekend of hard work—but it could take months, even years, of programming practice to get to that point.

Is it worth the time and effort to learn the basics of programming? The answer has to do with that somewhat ambiguously defined skill known as "computer literacy." As a minimum, one should know enough to use computers intelligently, to run and evaluate available software. If, beyond that, we know the basics of programming, we may be able to adapt other people's software to more closely suit our needs, or perhaps collaborate with a professional programmer to create more useful programs. But there is another reason for the language teacher to acquire at least some programming skills: as McCoy and Weibel (1983, 142) put it, "We must not leave the development of foreign language CAI materials to people who lack classroom experience." For us as language teachers to have a say in computer materials, we will need to understand what can be done (and what cannot), how it works, and how it could be made to work better. None of the existing software packages is, in itself, sufficient reason for buying a computer. The most useful foreign language applications will probably come from what we do, either as teacher/programmers or as computer-literate users who can adapt and modify the authoring systems or programs we buy.

A word of caution here. It is important not to underestimate the complexity inherent in a good piece of software. Two humbling aphorisms to keep in mind: "Only bad software is easy to write" (Botterell 1982), and "Software development is a very arcane art which very expert people do very poorly at."[1] Educational software, it is safe to say, is still a primarily amateur affair—we may be experts in many areas, but so far most of us are novices when it comes to programming.

That said, a word or two about the sort of project one should start working on. First, start small. Figure out how to manipulate a segment of language in an interesting way, then imagine how you could build on this manipulation to do something useful. Don't start off by trying to do a rehash of all those things we already do—that's how we got so many boring drills. One very successful firm in the educational game field, The Learning Company, gets its best ideas by letting its computer whizzes first explore ways in which the computer can do something particularly well, and then designing a program to take advantage of it. That's how a clever logic-circuitry game known as ROCKY'S BOOTS was born. (The user "moves" wires around and "connects" basic circuits of the sort that make computers work.) If we simply take our existing curriculum and computerize it, we will probably not come up with much.

8.2.1 BASIC

For most micro users, general-purpose programming languages will mean only one—BASIC. Wyatt (1983) estimates that 80 percent of educational software to date has been written in this language. The reason for this is simple enough: BASIC is usually the language that comes with the machine (not to be confused with machine language, those cryptic strings of ones and zeros), and thus there is no additional cost involved. It is a fairly simple language to learn to use, and has good "string handling" capabilities, referring to the way it deals with strings of characters, that is, words and sentences—obviously crucial for language use. There are different dialects of BASIC, but the language is for the most part fairly standardized.

When one looks at other languages, however, it seems unfortunate that the industry standard had to be BASIC. The design of the language tends to encourage untidy, unstructured programming, columns of cryptically numbered commands (detractors call it "spaghetti code") that can be very hard to read—even for the programmer, once a little time has gone by. BASIC does not lend itself, according to many seasoned programmers, to "elegant solutions."

8.2.2 Pascal

Pascal, by contrast, is a highly structured language, and for this reason is now the language of choice for teaching programming in colleges and universities. A Pascal program is transparently logical and easy to read, making heavy use of indentation to mark off parts within parts. But the real power of a language like Pascal lies in its use of procedures, subroutines that do all the work and that can be called up as needed by simply stating their procedure names. In Pascal, these names can have up to eight letters, and can thus be highly mnemonic. For example, the heart of a Pascal program that draws a simple picture of a house might look like this:

```
program house (output);
    begin
        walls;
        door;
        windows;
        roof;
    end.
```

Each of these words (*walls, doors,* etc.) is a procedure spelled out elsewhere in the program, wherein each has its own "begin" and "end" statements marking it off. The advantage of this procedural structure is that it is much clearer what the program does, and in what order. And if changes need to be made, they can be made within the appropriate procedure without affecting the rest of the program. Earlier versions of Pascal were not particularly well suited to string handling, but most versions now available for micros have built-in string functions; UCSD Pascal even has LOGO-like turtle graphics (see Section 8.2.3).

8.2.3 LOGO

LOGO is also a procedural language. It is usually thought of as a "children's language" for doing turtle graphics, which involves typing in simple commands that cause a blotch on the screen (the turtle) to move about and draw geometrical figures. This was what its designer, Seymour Papert, meant by letting "the child program the computer." Once the child has "taught" the turtle how to draw a square, for example, the turtle can use this knowledge (actually a procedure) to draw complicated patterns based on squares. Papert's idea has apparently caught on; drawing with LOGO has become very popular in this country, particularly in the elementary schools.

But LOGO is also a very powerful string handling language. In fact, in this respect it is much like LISP, the language traditionally used for natural language artificial intelligence work (see Section 8.2.4). Not only can LOGO "read in" and "type out" a sentence with the ease of BASIC, it uses built-in functions known as FIRST, LAST, BUTFIRST, and BUTLAST to provide easy access to the elements inside the sentence. (LISP has the same functions, but with considerably less mnemonic names: FIRST is "CAR," BUTFIRST is "CDR.") Suppose the input sentence (which we will call SENT) is "Mary had two little lambs." LOGO allows us to pick out any of its parts:

```
FIRST SENT [i.e. "do FIRST to the        Mary
            SENTence"]

LAST SENT                                lambs

BUTFIRST SENT                            had two little lambs

BUTLAST SENT                             Mary had two little

FIRST (BUTFIRST SENT)                    had

FIRST (BUTFIRST (BUTFIRST SENT))         two
```

It even allows us to separate individual letters from words within the sentence, giving us access to such things as inflectional endings:

```
FIRST (FIRST SENT)                   M

LAST (FIRST (BUTFIRST SENT))         d
```

85

Consider the following "natural language" program, which converts ordinary English words (EWORD) into pig latin (i.e., "igpay atinlay"):

```
1   TO PIGLATIN :EWORD

2   IF MEMBERP FIRST :EWORD [A E I O U]
        [OUTPUT WORD :EWORD "AY]

3   OUTPUT PIGLATIN WORD BUTFIRST :EWORD FIRST :EWORD

4   END
```

(The line numbers are only for reference, since LOGO does not use numbering.) What these four lines mean in simple English is the following:

1   Here is how TO do PIGLATIN to a variable we will call EWORD:

2   IF the FIRST element of EWORD is a MEMBER of the set [A E I O U], then OUTPUT as one WORD the combination of EWORD and the suffix "AY";

3   Otherwise, go back and try to do PIGLATIN again (i.e., starting in line 2) to the BUTFIRST of EWORD followed by the FIRST of EWORD;

4   The procedure PIGLATIN ends here.

Note that this little program, like human language, is recursive, since it calls itself in line 3. This means the program keeps restarting until the condition set up in the IF statement finally proves true—that is, when the first letter in EWORD turns out to be a vowel. Each time, the FIRST is peeled off the front and moved to the back. If EWORD were, for example, *splendid,* the process would go like this:

First pass	plendids
Second pass	lendidsp
Third pass	endidspl
Fourth pass	endidsplay

On the fourth try, the IF condition is met, the "AY" suffix is added, and the program is finished. (Of course it's all over in a matter of milliseconds.)

8.2.4 LISP

LISP is LOGO's big brother and is a radical departure from most other, "algebraic," languages. In LISP everything is a list (hence LISt-

Processing), and all "commands" are actually functions that relate or connect lists to other lists. The result is an elegant chaining and inter-mingling of symbols in a manner reminiscent (some feel) of the organizational patterns of the mind. It is thus understandably the favorite language of researchers in artificial intelligence. LISP is not linear (like BASIC), but can make connections in many different directions at once. It is recursive, meaning it can loop back and restart itself (as LOGO does in the PIGLATIN program). It has no "top" or "bottom" in the usual sense, but simply extends itself to encompass long and complex programs with virtually unfathomable depths of embedding within embedding. What's more, a LISP program can actually be designed to make corrections in itself as it "learns" more about the data. A sample of LISP code would not, in itself, be very revealing. One can set much of the flavor of LISP thinking, however, by considering any deeply embedded English sentence, such as (1), which is as grammatical as (2), but somewhat harder to parse because of the added layer of embedding:

(1)   The man the girl Peter thought was Mary said was Harry's brother turned out to be Ralph.

(2)   The man the girl said was Harry's brother turned out to be Ralph.

The full implications of LISP's characteristics are beyond the scope of this book. Its potential for CALL courseware, however, should be evident from the description of FAMILIA and QUESTIONS in earlier chapters, both of which are in LISP. As more and more efforts are made in the direction of "intelligent" CALL programs, programmers will turn increasingly to LISP. In the meantime, most CALL programmers will probably find LOGO easier to work with.

8.3 CAI AUTHORING LANGUAGES

Writing instructional programs from the ground up is clearly not for everyone. Estimates of the time it takes to produce good software run anywhere from 10 to 300 hours per hour of instruction. In part, the time invested depends on just how much of the "wheel" one has to reinvent each time. General-purpose languages lack many of the basic functions which are essential to CAI. For example, unless the programmer creates special input-editing routines, a BASIC or LOGO program will only accept input that is exactly the same as what the computer is expecting; typos, extra spaces, any sort of funny keypresses will be wrong. One way to get around this is to purchase ready-made subroutines which perform input-editing operations. Various "toolkit" programs are available for this purpose, such as the Applesoft Tool Kit or the MECC subroutine packages. A less complicated way to go about it is to buy a programming language especially designed for CAI.

8.3.1 PILOT

Although various authoring languages or systems have been developed (TICCIT, TUTOR, PLANIT), probably the best known is PILOT. With such a language, much of the work is done for you. To have PILOT print out a line of text requires only the command T (for Type); to input the student's response is just A (Accept). But the heart of PILOT's power is the Match command M. This command compares the student's response with a list of acceptable character strings or words to see if there is a match. Items being matched can range anywhere from an affix to a whole phrase. The following simple (if not silly) routine will demonstrate (the "!" means "or"):

```
T:    ?Cua'l is la forma ma's ra'pida de ir a Espana?

A:

M:    avion!avio'n!aeroplano!Iberia!TWA

TY:   Si', es cierto.

TN:   ?Co'mo?  Otra vez:
```

The last two lines are the two possible prefab responses, depending on whether the match succeeds or fails: TY (type if yes) or TN (type if no). The match will succeed if any of the words listed occurs anywhere in the student's response, even if they are embedded inside a longer word. Thus the unaccented form *avion* will correctly match in the following answer:

Yo prefiero los aviones.

While the "!" allows for a match with *any* of the items listed, occasionally we will want to match with *all* of them, as in

```
T:   Quels sont les couleurs du drapeau français?
A:
M:   rouge&blanc&bleu
```

Elements joined together by "&" will match in any order.

PILOT's matching ability facilitates the strategy known as "partial answer processing," discussed in Chapter 5. Instead of simply matching for the whole form, the programmer can use a series of matches to check for parts of the form, thus permitting some diagnosis of the error. It is a laborious process to program, and one filled with pitfalls, but if nothing else it gives the teacher/programmer a deep respect for the complexity of language. Suppose, for example, we were designing a program to practice Spanish past imperfect forms. These consist of three parts: the verb stem, the imperfect affix, and the person-marking suffix. In a form such as *comíamos,* "we used to eat," the three parts are *com-, -ía,* and *-mos,* respectively. Breaking the form down allows for the following series of "diagnostic" matches (again, line numbers are for reference):

```
1    M:   com

2    TN:  El radical no esta' bien.

3    JN:  *ANS1

4    M:   comi'a

5    TN:  Este verbo necesita "i'a" en el imperfecto.

6    JN:  *ANS1

7    M:   comi'amos

8    TN:  La terminacio'n no esta' bien.

9    JN:  *ANS1

10   TY:  Muy bien.
```

The command JN: *ANS1 is a "Jump" (if No) back to the beginning of the answer loop each time the match fails. Note that there are no "TYs" until the end. As each match in turn succeeds, analysis automatically falls into the next Match statement. Thus if *com* matches in line 1, the program proceeds to line 4 to check for *ía.* If this part is not present, the message in 5 is printed out and the program jumps back to try again. If *ía* is found, matching proceeds in line 7. If all matches succeed, none of the "No" commands is invoked, and only the last TY line is used.

As an alternative to partial answer processing, one could use the strategy of error anticipation (see Chapter 5). Instead of matching for parts of the correct answer, there could be a series of matches for expected wrong answers, with appropriate diagnostic messages. Remember, however, that neither approach is a very efficient way to write a program, since for each response to be processed a whole set of commands has to be created.

89

PILOT clearly offers several advantages for the novice programmer. For tasks such as those described, its code is simple and straightforward. The language has built-in input editing functions that clean up student responses of extraneous keypresses and allow for reasonable typos to be overlooked. (This feature can be turned off if the programmer wants only exactly spelled forms to be accepted.) SuperPilot, an expanded version of PILOT available for the Apple II, allows for the addition of color graphics, sound effects (including music), the creation of foreign language character sets, and even incorporates built-in commands for controlling videotape or videodisc players.

The simplicity of PILOT, however, is both an advantage and a limitation. Many routines either cannot be done with PILOT or can only be done in a somewhat clumsy fashion. I have argued elsewhere (Underwood 1981b) that one could use PILOT for a rudimentary sort of conversational program, with computer questions and student answers. As I pointed out, however, this only works on the assumption that the program checks a part of the answer (the verb form, perhaps) and blithely ignores the rest; otherwise, the string of matching routines would get out of hand. Once the programmer acquires a certain amount of expertise and wants to break out of the drill-and-practice format, the limitations of PILOT will be evident.[2]

8.3.2 EnBASIC

EnBASIC ("Enhanced BASIC"; cf. Tenczar et al. 1983) in many ways incorporates the advantages of PILOT with the flexibility and power of a general programming language. EnBASIC is a supplement to standard BASIC which provides a number of special CAI routines. It has a built-in match command similar to PILOT's, automatically edits student input, and allows for the creation of special character sets (accent marks, etc.). In addition, it has a "Markup" command that can be invoked to automatically provide visual "pattern markup" of the DASHER type. Although, as we have seen, pattern markup is not an entirely revealing process for the student, certainly the combination of "matches" and "markups" gives the teacher a potentially powerful tool.

8.4 FOREIGN LANGUAGE AUTHORING SYSTEMS

The difference between a CAI system such as EnBASIC and a foreign language authoring system is that the latter requires no programming at all, only the insertion of foreign language data. These are sometimes called "template systems"—the shape is there, but the content is missing. A good template system will require no special skills for the teacher other than the ability to type on a computer. This means an enormous saving in time—

both the time needed to learn the system and the time it takes to produce courseware with it. Of course it also means that the system will do only what it was designed to do, nothing more, nothing less.

DASHER (Pusack 1983b) is a good example of such a system. Since its operation was described in some detail in Chapter 5, I will not repeat that description here. The advantage of such a system is that teachers who want to produce their own tailor-made drill-and-practice materials can do so quickly and painlessly, and benefit from the relatively sophisticated answer-processing techniques that are built in. It can be used for any language, at any level, and it can be used over and over again. If, however, one decides that there is more to language learning than drill and practice (or indeed, that drill is of little or no use), systems such as DASHER will not offer a solution.[3]

8.5 READY-MADE COURSEWARE

We have seen several examples of off-the-shelf courseware in Chapters 5 and 6. Some of them are at least marginally useful, many of them are not. As more and more software becomes available, the task of separating worthwhile programs from the rest will become both more important and more difficult. Survey reviews such as Harrison (1983) and Culley and Mulford (1983) will be of considerable help. So, too, the increasing number of separate reviews in such journals as *Electronic Learning, School MicroWare Reviews,* etc. (see Appendix).

Most teachers, though, will want to try the programs out before they buy them. Publishers have still not worked out a standard policy regarding previewing software. Although we would never buy a textbook without requesting an examination copy, this is so far standard procedure for ordering courseware, since publishers are understandably reluctant to mail their expensive diskettes for free trials and thus risk having them pirated. Demonstration disks such as the CONDUIT demo (Appendix) are a big help. We should be seeing more of these as larger publishing firms begin marketing programs on a somewhat grander scale than the mostly "cottage industry" efforts so far. One way teachers often get to try out software is at one of the "hands on" sessions at professional conventions or workshops.

8.5.1 Evaluating Software

Even when we do get our hands on, the question remains: What are we looking for? A number of schemes have been proposed for evaluating CALL software: Culley and Mulford 1983, Strei 1983, Hope et al. 1984, among others. Many of the criteria suggested are simply common sense: Does it run without getting stuck? Are there any language errors? Are the instructions clear? And so forth. Two more or less general criteria are clearly crucial, however, and have much to do with everything we have been saying here: (1) Does the program make good use of the computer? and (2) Is the program pedagogically sound and worthwhile? Let us consider what these two questions mean.

8.5.1.1 Does the Program Make Good Use of the Computer?

"Good use of the computer" goes back to our basic rule that computers should not be used to do things that could be done just as well, if not better, with a book, a ditto, or a flashcard. To answer this question, one clearly needs to know what computers can do. Branching is a good example. A game such as MYSTERY HOUSE or ADVENTURE is exciting largely because it is the user who determines what happens at each step. This is a novel experience, different from either reading or watching a movie. A computer is also very good at "remembering" large quantities of information, which can then be recalled instantly. STORYBOARD and CLOZE-MASTER make good use of this feature.

More important, a computer is capable of those intricate and multi-layered calculations that bewilder the human brain precisely because they involve handling so many facts at the same time. In artificial intelligence a computer is programmed to make decisions on the basis of what it "knows," i.e., stored knowledge. When many decisions are made in a very short time, the computer appears "intelligent." By contrast, a program that requires very little decision making, one that needs only to decide, for example, whether the student's choice of the letter "B" on the keyboard matches the "B" in the program, seems anything but smart. Most CAI is unfortunately still in this latter category, and in that sense it obviously does not make good use of the computer.

"Good use of the computer" also means taking advantage of the computer's potential for being flexible and "open-minded." A good program should be able to guess which word the student meant (through input editing), and then decide if the answer is close enough to count. For example, the French program described in Holmes (1980) checks wrong answers to see if the first two letters are right, in which case the student is asked if there is a typo. Likewise, a good program will somehow be able to help the student figure out what went wrong—and not simply spit out the answer. This means incorporating some sort of escape routine for which the student types "help" or "H" or the like. One program counts the time the student takes to respond after each question, and if too much time (say 20 seconds) elapses, it prints out a reminder, "Type H if you need help" (cf. Collett 1981, 171). However, says Marty, we must not give too much help without it being asked for, but rather make many different kinds of assistance available, and let the students decide what kind and how much they need (Marty 1981, 31).

Flexibility means having plenty of options at every step: allowing students to interrupt at any point, jump back or forward to other exercises, without forcing them to go through a whole exercise just to get to the next one. In fact, on each item the student should always have the option of either typing or skipping it. Finally, when students have asked for help, the program will return them afterwards to where they left off.

There is also a certain amount of computer etiquette which should be standard by now: Generous use of blank space (it's free, after all) to make text easier to read, timed pauses to avoid pressuring the user, real accent marks instead of apostrophes and other strange characters after the letters,[4] and, of course, unambiguous instructions at every point (example: "Press RETURN," not "Type RETURN"). Needless to say, the program should never require any instructions beyond those that appear on the screen ("OK, who's got the instruction manual now?"). Finally, the program should respect the user as a human being, by being polite and helpful, never demanding, boring, or cute. "The success of computerized instruction depends on the student's regarding the computer system not as a tyrannical taskmaster, but rather as a tireless and resourceful tutor always ready to help when needed" (Marty and Myers 1975, 150).

8.5.1.2 Is the Program Pedagogically Sound and Worthwhile?

This second question is the province of language teachers. Does the program do anything that will help our students accomplish the goals we have set out for them? Of course here much will hinge on the nature of those goals and how we have defined them. The discussion in Part One was obviously intended to convince the reader that we should aim at fluency rather than accuracy, at "communicative competence" rather than the mechanical mastery of grammatical detail. Grammar of course must be learned. We have argued, however, that true acquisition comes not from conscious manipulation of rules but rather from *using* them, and hearing them used, in meaningful situations.

Where does this leave computers? There are two points of view on the question. According to one, the role of computers will be precisely to aid in "learning," to provide the means for the conscious manipulation of rules (such as drill and practice), leaving communicative activities for the classroom. For those who espouse this view, the question of pedagogical value is reduced to determining how efficiently, effectively, and smoothly the program drills the student.

The other point of view, the one that I have tried to make a case for here, is that such drill-and-practice activities may well be effective for "learning," in this sense, but that such learning probably plays only a rather limited and marginal role in the process whereby one becomes able to actually use the language to communicate. In this sense, then, strictly learning-centered computer programs will be little different from flashcards, pattern drill, or the memorization of paradigms: they will be of only marginal value in the preparation of our students, and thus would hardly justify the considerable investment of time and money they require. What is worse, drill and practice, once the novelty wears off, may actually prove to have negative effects—recall the detrimental effects of the language lab, particularly on the better students (see Section 4.1). I have argued, furthermore, that it is simply not the case that drill and practice is "all that computers can do"—Chapter 6 provides many examples of useful alternatives.

For those of us who subscribe to the latter point of view, evaluation of software is in one sense simplified. Since most of the available programs are of the drill-and-practice sort, we can focus our attention on a few. The question of worth can then be directed much more to the basic pedagogical issues so often repeated in this book: Does the program provide practice in using language instead of merely manipulating it? Does it provide context for the linguistic material used? Does the student have any control over the content of the lesson? Does the program use the target language exclusively? In the end the mark of a worthwhile program will always be that it emphasizes useful linguistic content more than programming sophistication.

The bottom line on buying a ready-made program is this: if the package cannot be modified or adapted in any way by the teacher, it had better be very, very good. Flaws that are only mildly annoying the first time through become amazingly irritating after the fifth run. Our students are not dumb. Already they are tiring of video games, which only proves they are demanding (if not discriminating) consumers of technology. If we make them sit in a booth somewhere in front of a screen and force them to trudge through a boring, silly, or trivial exercise, we will very soon start reliving the nightmare of the Great Language Lab Episode, when the key issue became not pedagogy but vandalism.

8.6 CALL: PROS AND CONS

Why do computer-assisted language learning in the first place? We are not yet in a position to answer, "Because it increases our students' proficiency in the language." There is still very little experimental evidence one way or the other. One study on CAI, although not specifically in foreign languages, could find "no significant impact on achievement" (Maggarell 1978). There is some evidence that computer work may be effective for remedial or tutorial work for students with special problems or needing extra help. Andrews (1973) found that the greatest gain among those students using CALL for French, when compared with a similar control group, was made by students who had scored low on the pretest given before the study began. Students in larger classes apparently find that CALL is a way of getting individual attention, especially with systems where the student can communicate with the teacher/author through the computer's "mail" system (in which case, note, the attention is from a human, not the computer). Students can set their own pace and work at their own schedule. And, at least so far, they seem to think it's fun.

It may very well turn out that the biggest advantage of using CALL software is a side effect, the dialog that occurs in front of the screen rather than on it. Many observers of educational computing have noted a decidedly social effect, a tendency to band together to try to "beat the machine." As we have noted, when the program communicates with the user in the target language, this off-screen dialog quickly begins imitating the program, so that the users themselves unwittingly begin providing each other with real language practice. We would do well to keep this effect in mind when we consider where and how our computers are to be used; sealing students off in hermetic booths in the fashion of the language lab may be a serious mistake.

For the skeptic, CALL has plenty of drawbacks. The biggest one, of course, is the quality of the software, which is what this book is primarily about. The other big problem is cost. Although many early programs ran on existing university hardware, costs in computer time and materials development often proved prohibitive. Stanford's successful CALL Russian program had to be scrapped after it was found that the course was costing more than three times as much as a conventional course taught by instructors (Nelson et al. 1976, 30n). A survey of college foreign language departments made in 1978–79 found that the most common reason given for not venturing into computer-assisted instruction was "cost-effectiveness" (Olsen 1980). Although the microcomputer has certainly altered the picture, there is no denying that cost is still a problem.

Another cause for skepticism is more subtle—the language teacher's natural and understandable tendency to regard computer technology with a mixture of anxiety and mystification, accompanied by the conviction that somehow machines don't belong in the humanities. Then, too, there is the vague suspicion that what the computer people have in mind is somehow replacing teachers. On this last point Decker argues, "[The computer] should be able to replace us as any useful machine does for given tasks—in order to free our time in the course to do what only a human being can do" (Decker 1976, 263).

Computers are also thought to be "rigid and inhuman." Obviously that depends entirely on the way they have been programmed: " 'Rigid and inhuman' computer systems," argues Nelson (1974, 12), "are the creation of rigid and inhuman people." Anyway, why pick on computers? Are not toasters, or bathtubs, "cold and inhuman"? If we are going to be Luddites, why not start with something truly inhuman and vicious, like the automobile?

All right, the skeptic says, so the computer is just another (possibly useful) machine. But who has the time to get involved in learning all this CALL stuff? Time is a real problem: "No other teaching technique purports to put a practical tool directly into our hands, yet requires such an investment of time to learn how to use" (Hope et al. 1984, 5). Yet even time is relative. It takes time to learn to type, or to drive a car. Using a computer will soon be no less common and, we hope, nearly as simple.

A more serious question, perhaps, is what will happen if we (foreign language teachers) do *not* get involved with computers. We are already seeing some of the effects. Both hardware and software producers are promoting techniques that any language teacher would consider highly questionable, at best. A priceless example of what happens when we are not consulted is an apparatus I saw being demonstrated at a statewide foreign language conference in California. The device was a voice recognition system which could be "trained" to recognize certain words. The claim was that it would be useful for foreign language pronunciation practice. Students would speak into the mike and the program would either accept their pronunciation as being "on target" or invite them to try again. The only catch was that "on target" did not mean "approximating native pronunciation," but rather only that the pronunciation was comparable to the first time the student spoke that particular word into the system, when it was being trained to recognize his or her particular voice. Conclusion: the student's pronunciation would only be "right" if it never improved! (The "theory" behind all this, according to the salesman, was that student pronunciation always tends to get sloppy as time goes by.)

Whether we want to get into it or not, CALL will not go away. Software will be produced anyway, and not necessarily in a way that will be useful to us or to our students. Bad software may well have the effect of turning people against the language profession, and ours is not a profession that can stand much bad publicity. This is clearly an opportunity, a chance to improve language teaching, raise the proficiency level of our students (and, not incidentally, attract more students)—or to fumble and finally drop the ball, as we did so dramatically following sputnik.

NOTES TO CHAPTER 8

1. Douglas van Houweling, Vice-Provost of Carnegie-Mellon University, quoted in the *Chronicle of Higher Education,* March 30, 1983, p. 11.

2. For a more detailed discussion of the advantages and disadvantages of PILOT, see Wyatt 1983.

3. Hope 1982 discusses an experiment with using DASHER to develop a set of French materials.

4. The dot-matrix printer used to produce the samples in this book unfortunately lacked this capability.

Appendix:
Resources for Computer Users

The following is a list of books and journals that may be helpful to the foreign language teacher interested in knowing more about computer-assisted language learning. For further reading, see the sources cited in References, Part Two.

1. General Books on Computers

McWilliams, Peter (1983) *The Personal Computer Book*. New York: Ballantine Books/Random House.

Probably the best introductory book on computers. Amusing, informative, updated every few months. Makes specific recommendations on hardware.

Glossbrenner, Alfred (1984) *How to Buy Software: The Master Guide to Picking the Right Program*. New York: St. Martin's Press.

Best overall guide to software of all kinds: what's useful and what isn't, and how to tell the difference. Covers everything that runs on personal computers (648 pages).

2. Books on CAI

Bork, A. (1981) *Learning with Computers*. Bedford, Massachusetts: Digital Press.

Basic text on psychological principles behind computer-assisted instruction.

Papert, Seymour (1980) *Mindstorms: Children, Computers, and Powerful Ideas*. New York: Basic Books.

Premises behind LOGO, and insightful criticism of the classic CAI approach to kids and computers.

3. Books on CALL

Culley, Gerald R., and George W. Mulford (1983) (eds.) *Foreign Language Teaching Programs for Microcomputers: A Volume of Reviews*. Newark, Delaware: University of Delaware. ERIC Document number 234 648.

Descriptions of CALL software as reviewed by a group of foreign language teachers in the summer of 1982. Available from ERIC Document Reproduction Service, P.O. Box 190, Arlington, Virginia 22210.

Higgins, John, and Tim Johns (1984) *Computers in Language Learning*. Reading, Massachusetts: Addison-Wesley.

Excellent discussion of the alternatives to the "wrong-try-again" approach, with many examples of actual programs developed or being developed by the British Council.

Hope, G. R., H. Taylor, and J. P. Pusack (forthcoming 1984) *Using Computers in Language Teaching.* Arlington, Virginia: Center for Applied Linguistics.

Authors take a more traditional programmed-instruction approach to CALL, tend to regard "communicative" CALL as impractical. Useful annotated bibliography on a wide range of CALL literature.

Kenning, M. J., and M. M. Kenning (1984) *An Introduction to Computer Assisted Language Teaching.* Reading, Massachusetts: Addison-Wesley.

A "how-to" book for those who want to try their hand at programming simple CALL programs (in BASIC).

4. On Artificial Intelligence

Winston, Patrick (1977) *Artificial Intelligence.* Reading, Massachusetts: Addison-Wesley.

Introduction to the principles of AI and programming in LISP.

5. Journals

CALICO Journal
  Computer Assisted Language Learning and Instruction Consortium
  233 SFLC, Brigham Young University, Provo UT 84602.
  [The only journal devoted exclusively to CALL]

The Computing Teacher
  Department of Computer and Information Science
  University of Oregon, Eugene, OR 97403

Electronic Learning
  902 Sylvan Avenue, Englewood Cliffs, NJ 07632

Foreign Language Annals
  American Council on the Teaching of Foreign Languages (ACTFL)
  385 Warburton Avenue, Hastings-on-Hudson, NY 10706

Journal of Courseware Review
  P.O. Box 28426, San Jose, CA 95159

MicroSIFT News
  Northwest Regional Educational Laboratory
  300 S.W. Sixth Avenue, Portland, OR 97204

NECTFL Newsletter
  Northeast Conference on the Teaching of Foreign Languages
  P.O. Box 623, Middlebury, VT 05753

Pipeline
    CONDUIT, P.O. Box 388, Iowa City, IA 52240
    [Ask for their free CALL demo disk]

School MicroWare
    Dresden Associates
    P.O. Box 246, Dresden, ME 04342

TESOL Newsletter
    Teachers of English to Speakers of Other Languages
    202 D.C. Transit Building, Georgetown University
    Washington, DC 20057
    [Has regular column, "On Line," on CALL]

References

Part One: Linguistics and Language Teaching

Asher, James J., J. Kusudo, and R. de la Torre (1974) "Learning a second language through commands: The second field test," *Modern Language Journal* 58:24–32.

Axelrod, Joseph (1966) *The Education of the Modern Foreign Language Teacher for American Schools.* New York: Modern Language Association.

Benseler, David P., and Renate A. Schulz (1980) "Methodological trends in college foreign language instruction," *Modern Language Journal* 64:88–96.

Blair, Robert W. (1982) *Innovative Approaches to Language Teaching.* Rowley, Massachusetts: Newbury House.

Bolinger, Dwight, et al. (1966) *Modern Spanish: A Project of the Modern Language Association* (2nd ed.). New York: Harcourt.

Chastain, Kenneth (1976) *Developing Second-Language Skills: Theory to Practice* (2nd ed.). Chicago: Rand McNally.

Chomsky, Noam (1957) *Syntactic Structures.* The Hague: Mouton.

Chomsky, Noam (1959) "Review of B. F. Skinner, Verbal Behavior," *Language* 35:26–58.

Chomsky, Noam (1966) "Linguistic theory," in R. Mead, Jr. (ed.), *Reports of the Working Committees, Northeast Conference on the Teaching of Foreign Languages* (New York: MLA Materials Center).

Chomsky, Noam (1969) "Some observations on the teaching of language," *Pedagogic Reporter* 21.2:5–6, 13.

Curran, Charles A. (1972) *Counseling-Learning: A Whole-Person Model for Education.* New York: Grune and Stratton.

DeSauze, Emile B. (1931) *The Cleveland Plan for the Teaching of Modern Languages, with Special Reference to Spanish.* Philadelphia: John C. Winston.

Diller, Karl C. (1978) *The Language Teaching Controversy.* Rowley, Massachusetts: Newbury House.

Dulay, Heidi C., and Marina K. Burt (1977) "Remarks on creativity in language acquisition," in M. Burt, H. Dulay, and M. Finocchiaro (eds.), *Viewpoints on English as a Second Language* (New York: Regents), 95–126.

Fries, Charles C. (1945) *Teaching and Learning English as a Foreign Language.* Ann Arbor: University of Michigan Press.

Gary, Judith Olmsted, and Norman Gary (1981a) "Comprehension-based language instruction: Theory," in Winitz, 1981, 332–342.

Gary, Norman, and Judith Olmsted Gary (1981b) "Comprehension-based language instruction: Practice," in Winitz, 1981, 343–357.

Gattegno, Caleb (1976) *The Common Sense of Teaching Foreign Languages.* New York: Educational Solutions.

Harvey, John H. T. (1982) "A communicational approach: Games II," in Blair, 1982, 204–213.

Hatch, Evelyn (1979) "Simplified input and second language acquisition." Unpublished paper presented to the annual meeting of the Linguistic Society of America, Los Angeles.

Hester, Ralph M. (1970) (ed.) *Teaching a Living Language.* New York: Harper and Row.

Hockett, Charles (1958) *A Course in Modern Linguistics.* New York: Macmillan.

Jakobovits, Leon (1968) "Implications of recent psycholinguistic developments for the teaching of a second language," *Language Learning* 18.1/2:89–109.

James, Charles J. (1983) *Practical Applications of Research in Foreign Language Teaching.* Lincolnwood, Illinois: National Textbook Company.

Kelley, Louis G. (1969) *Twenty-Five Centuries of Language Teaching.* Rowley, Massachusetts: Newbury House.

Krashen, Stephen D. (1982) *Principles and Practice in Second Language Acquisition.* Oxford: Pergamon Press.

Krashen, Stephen D. (1983) "Applications of psycholinguistic research to the classroom," in James, 1983, 51–66.

Krashen, Stephen D., and Tracy D. Terrell (1983) *The Natural Approach: Language Acquisition in the Classroom.* Oxford: Pergamon Press.

Lenard, Yvone (1970) "Methods and materials, techniques and the teacher," in Hester (1970).

Littlewood, William (1981) *Communicative Language Teaching: An Introduction.* Cambridge, England: University of Cambridge Press.

Newmark, Leonard (1966) "How not to interfere with language learning," *International Journal of Applied Linguistics* 32.12.

Rivers, Wilga M. (1968) *Teaching Foreign Language Skills.* Chicago: University of Chicago Press.

Rivers, Wilga M. (1976) *Speaking in Many Tongues* (2nd ed.). Rowley, Massachusetts: Newbury House.

Stevick, Earl (1976) *Memory, Meaning and Method: Some Psychological Perspectives on Language Learning.* Rowley, Massachusetts: Newbury House.

Stevick, Earl (1980) *Teaching Languages: A Way and Ways.* Rowley, Massachusetts: Newbury House.

Stevick, Earl (1982) *Teaching and Learning Languages.* Cambridge, England: University of Cambridge Press.

Terrell, Tracy D. (1977) "A natural approach to second language acquisition and learning," *Modern Language Journal* 61:325–326. Reprinted in Blair, 1982, 160–173.

Terrell, Tracy D. (1982) "The natural approach: An update," *Modern Language Journal* 66:121–132.

Winitz, Harris (1981) *Native Language and Foreign Language Acquisition.* New York: New York Academy of Sciences.

References

Winitz, Harris, and James A. Reeds (1973) "Rapid acquisition of a foreign language (German) by the avoidance of speaking," *International Review of Applied Linguistics in Language Teaching* 10.1/4:295–317.

Wolfe, David L. (1967) "Some theoretical aspects of language learning and language teaching," *Language Learning* 17.3/4:173–188.

Part Two: Computers and Language Teaching

Adams, E. N., H. W. Morrison, and J. M. Reddy (1968) "Conversation with a computer as a technique of language instruction," *Modern Language Journal* 52.1:3–16.

Ahl, David H. (1975) "Computers in language arts," in O. Lecarme and R. Lewis (eds.), *Computers in Education* (Amsterdam: North-Holland).

Allen, John R. (1971) "Two routines for use in CAI language programs," *Computers and the Humanities* 6.2:125–128.

Allen, John R. (1972) "Individualizing foreign language instruction with computers at Dartmouth," *Foreign Language Annals* 5.3:348–349.

Allen, Edward D., and Rebecca M. Valette (1977) *Classroom Techniques: Foreign Languages and English as a Second Language.* New York: Harcourt Brace Jovanovich.

Andrews, Charles S. (1973) "An investigation of the use of computer-assisted instruction in French as an adjunct to classroom instruction." Unpublished doctoral dissertation, Florida State University.

Barrutia, Richard (1970) "Two approaches to self-instructional language study: Computerized foreign language instruction," *Hispania* 53.3:361–371.

Bolt, Richard H. (1968) "Computer-assisted Socratic instruction," in Orr (ed.), 1968, 90–95.

Botterell, Art (1982) "Which micro for me? A guide for the prospective user," *Educational Computer Magazine* 2.1:51.

Boyle, Thomas A. (1976) "Computer-mediated testing: A branched program achievement test," *Modern Language Journal* 60.8:428–440.

Cerri, Stefano, and Joost Breuker (1981) "A rather intelligent language teacher," *Studies in Language Learning* 3.1:182–192.

Collett, M. J. (1981) "Examples of applications of computers to modern language study; Part 2: Storage and retrieval: The development of an index of learning resources," *System* 9.1:35–40.

Culley, Gerald R., and George W. Mulford (1983) *Foreign Language Teaching Programs for Microcomputers: A Volume of Reviews.* Newark, Delaware: University of Delaware.

Decker, Henry W. (1976) "Computer-aided instruction in French syntax," *Modern Language Journal* 60.5/6:263–267.

Dessruisseaux, Paul (1983) "Lack of computer programs slows use, humanists say," *Chronicle of Higher Education,* February 2, 1983, 10.

Epting, Richard S., and J. Donald Bowen (1979) "Resurrecting the language lab for teaching listening comprehension and related skills," in M. Celce-Murcia and L. McIntosh (eds.), *Teaching English as a Second or Foreign Language* (Rowley, Massachusetts: Newbury House), 74–79.

Gale, Larrie E. (1983) "Montevidisco: An anecdotal history of an interactive videodisc," *CALICO Journal* 1.1:42–46. 1983.

Harrison, John (1983) "Foreign language software: 1983. What? Where? How good?," *Northeast Conference Newsletter* 13, 26–30.

Hart, Robert S. (1981) "Language study and the PLATO system," *Studies in Language Learning* 3.1:1–24.

Higgins, John (1983a) "Computer assisted language learning," *Language Teaching* 16.2:102–114.

Higgins, John (1983b) "Can computers teach?," *CALICO Journal* 1.2:4–6.

Higgins, John, and Tim Johns (1984) *Computers in Language Learning*. Reading, Massachusetts: Addison-Wesley.

Holmes, Glyn (1980) "A contextualized vocabulary learning drill for French," *Computers and the Humanities* 14.2:105–111.

Hope, Geoffrey (1982) "Elementary French computer-assisted instruction," *Foreign Language Annals* 15.5:347–353.

Hope, G. R., H. Taylor, and J. P. Pusack (1984) *Using Computers in Language Teaching*. Arlington, Virginia: Center for Applied Linguistics.

Keating, Raymond F. (1963) *A Study of the Effectiveness of Language Laboratories*. New York: Institute of Administrative Research, Teachers College, Columbia University.

Leonard, George B. (1968) *Education and Ecstasy*. New York: Delacorte Press.

Levien, Roger E. (1972) *The Emerging Technology: Instructional Use of the Computer in Higher Education*. New York: McGraw-Hill.

Loritz, Donald (1984) "Computer-assisted diagnosis and instruction in L2 phonetics." Paper given at TESOL '84, Houston, Texas.

Maggarell, Jack (1978) "Computer teaching systems: Little impact on achievement," *Chronicle of Higher Education* 17.5:5.

Marcus, Stephen (1981) "Teaching writing skills using computers," *Proceedings of the 1981 Western Educational Computing Conference*, San Francisco, California, November 19–20, 1981.

Marty, Fernand (1981) "Reflections on the use of computers in second-language acquisition," *Studies in Language Learning* 3.1:25–53.

Marty, Fernand, and M. Keith Myers (1975) "Computerized instruction in second-language acquisition," *Studies in Language Learning* 1.1:132–152.

McCoy, Ingeborg H., and David M. Weible (1983) "Foreign languages and the new media: The videodisc and the microcomputer," in Charles J. James (ed.), *Practical Applications of Research in Foreign Language Teaching*. Lincolnwood, Illinois: National Textbook Company.

Meredith, R. Alan (1981) "Review of Practicando Español con la Manzana II," *Journal of Courseware Review* 1.1:71–74.

Morrison, H. W., and E. N. Adams (1968) "Pilot study of CAI laboratory in German," *Modern Language Journal* 52.5:279–287.

Nelson, Theodor H. (1970) "No more teachers' dirty looks," *Computer Decisions*, September 1970. Reprinted in Nelson, 1974.

Nelson, Theodor H. (1974) *Computer Lib*. Chicago: Hugo's Book Service.

103

Nelson, G. E., Jean R. Ward, Samuel H. Desch, and Roy Kaplow (1976) "Two new strategies for computer-assisted language instruction," *Foreign Language Annals* 9.1:28–37.

Odendaal, M. (1982) "Second language learning and computer-assisted language instruction (CALI)," *INTUS News* (Stellenbosch University) 6.1:37–45.

Olsen, Solveig (1980) "Foreign language departments and computer-assisted instruction: A survey," *Modern Language Journal* 64.3:341–349.

Ornstein, Jacob (1970) "Once more: Programmed instruction in the language field: The state of the art," *Language Learning* 20.2:213–222.

Orr, William D. (ed.) (1968) *Conversational Computers.* New York: John Wiley.

Otto, Sue K., and James P. Pusack (1983) "Stringing us along: Programming for foreign language CAI," *CALICO Journal* 1.2:26–33.

Papert, Seymour (1980) *Mindstorms: Children, Computers and Powerful Ideas.* New York: Basic Books.

Paulston, Christina Bratt (1980) "Structural pattern drills: A classification," *Foreign Language Annals* 4.2:187–193.

Phillips, Robert (1981) *Practicando Español con la Manzana II.* Iowa City, Iowa: CONDUIT.

Pusack, James (1981) "Computer-assisted instruction in foreign language," *Pipeline* 6.2:5–8, 10.

Pusack, James P. (1983a). "Answer-processing and error correction in foreign language CAI," *System* 11.1:53–64.

Pusack, James P. (1983b) *DASHER: An Answer Processor for Language Study.* Iowa City, Iowa: CONDUIT.

Putnam, Constance E. (1983) "Foreign language instructional technology: The state of the art," *CALICO Journal* 1.1:35–41.

Rivers, Wilga M. (1981) *Teaching Foreign Language Skills* (2nd ed.). Chicago: University of Chicago Press.

Rockart, John F., and Michael S. S. Morton (1975) *Computers and the Learning Process in Higher Education.* New York: McGraw-Hill.

Rosenbaum, Peter S. (1969) "The computer as a learning environment for foreign language instruction," *Foreign Language Annals* 2.4:457–465.

Sanders, Ruth (1983) "'Intelligent' games for German language teaching," in *Foreign Language Instructional Technology Conference Proceedings,* 21–24 September, 1982 (Monterey, California: Defense Language Institute).

Schaeffer, Robert H. (1981) "Meaningful practice on the computer: Is it possible?" *Foreign Language Annals* 14.2:133–137.

Smith, Philip D., Jr. (1970) *A Comparison of the Cognitive and Audiolingual Approaches to Foreign Language Instruction: The Pennsylvania Foreign Language Project.* Philadelphia: Center for Curriculum Development.

Staton, Jana (1983) "Dialogue journals: A new tool for teaching communication," *ERIC/CLL News Bulletin* 6.2:1–2, 6.

Strei, Jerry (1983) "Format for the evaluation of courseware used in computer-assisted language instruction (CALI)," *CALICO Journal* 1.2:43–46.

Suppes, Patrick (1966) "The use of computers in education," *Scientific American* 215.3:206–220.

Tenczar Paul, Stanley Smith, and Allen Avner (1983) *EnBASIC Authoring System.* Wentworth, New Hampshire: COMPress.

Terry, Robert M. (1977) "Students work with MONIQUE and learn French," *Foreign Language Annals* 10.2:191–197.

Turner, Ronald C. (1970) "CARLOS: Computer-assisted instruction in Spanish," *Hispania* 53:249–252.

Tuttle, Harry G. (1983) "Programming/evaluating second language CAI," *Foreign Language Annals* 16.1:35–39.

Underwood, John (1981a) "Chomsky, DeSauze, and the computer: A humanistic approach to the teaching of language." Unpublished doctoral dissertation, University of California, Los Angeles.

Underwood, John (1981b) "Using PILOT for 'conversational' foreign language programs," *Educational Computer Magazine* 1.4:33, 50.

Underwood, John (1982) "Simulated conversation as a CAI strategy," *Foreign Language Annals* 15.3:209–212.

Weibel, David (1980) "Teaching reading skills through linguistic redundancy," *Foreign Language Annals* 13.6:487–493.

Weibel, David (1983) "The foreign language teacher as courseware author," *CALICO Journal* 1.1:62–64.

Weischedel, Ralph M., Wilfried M. Woge, and Mark James (1978) "An artificial intelligence approach to language instruction," *Artificial Intelligence* 10.3:225–240.

Weizenbaum, Joseph (1976) *Computer Power and Human Reason: From Judgment to Calculation.* San Francisco: W.H. Freeman.

Winograd, Terry (1972) *Understanding Natural Language.* New York: Academic Press.

Winograd, Terry (1983) *Language as a Cognitive Process. Volume I: Syntax.* Reading, Massachusetts: Addison-Wesley.

Wyatt, David H. (1983) "Three major approaches to developing computer-assisted language learning materials for microcomputers," *CALICO Journal* 1.2:34–38.

Index

Alphabetical order is letter-by-letter; compound headings of two or more words are treated as single entities. Names of computer programs or languages are given in upper case. In cases of multiple authorship of works cited, only the first author's name is listed.